Becoming Edith:
The Education of a
Hidden Child

By

Edith Mayer Cord

The Wordsmithy, LLC
New Milford, New Jersey
2008

Becoming Edith:
The Education of a Hidden Child

Copyright© 2008 by Edith Mayer Cord
ISBN 978-1-935110-01-9

Designed by The Wordsmithy, LLC

Published by The Wordsmithy, LLC
P.O. Box 224
New Milford, NJ 07646

This book is dedicated to my father

S.J. (Adolf) Mayer
Deported from Drancy, France
9.11.1942
via convoi No. 31

to my brother

Kurt (Mordechai) Mayer
Deported from Drancy, France
8.31.1942
via convoi No. 26

and to all those murdered during the Shoah.

Edith Mayer, age 7½, in Vienna, 1936.

ACKNOWLEDGMENTS

This book started as notes because my children—in particular, my daughter Emily—wanted me to write down my "stories." It took form through the encouragement of many friends and relatives, but especially because of the unceasing support of my lifelong friend Leon Vermont. It became a book with the help of my editor, Jeanette Friedman, who has now become my friend. It was her skill and her dedication that helped me to complete this difficult and sometimes painful task.

I should add that the young audiences I have been privileged to address have led me to write down my story for future generations. It is my hope that they will be inspired to meet the challenges they may face in order to build a fulfilling life and a better world.

Edith Mayer Cord
Columbia, MD
Spring 2008

ODE TO ...

It is the cheapest commodity.
It is freely available. It doesn't cost a penny.
Everyone can give it away.
Those who receive it feel blessed by it and supremely happy.
It can be given to old and young, to men and women, during good times and bad ones.
It doesn't depend on the state of the economy, nor is location an issue.
It is available to everyone, regardless of circumstances.

In spite of all this, it is in short supply.
People do not give it out freely.
Yet everyone needs it.
Everyone suffers from its lack.
It can take many forms and can be adapted to the giver, or to the receiver.
Still it is in short supply.

Why is everyone so stingy with it?
Why isn't it the most widespread and freely given of all gifts?
It heals, it gives pleasure and happiness, it renews energy and brings peace and harmony.
The young thrive on it and the old live longer.
Both the giver and the receiver benefit.

It can take the form of goodwill toward all men
Or it can create deep bonds between beings attuned to each other.
Beings can vibrate in such harmony that they attain profound joy
And experience the oneness we all yearn for.

Why isn't there more of it?
And what is it?

LOVE

INTRODUCTION

These are some of the stories I told my children as they were growing up. This story is for them, and for other children, too—especially children raised under dire straits.

This book may also serve as a record of one person's experiences during the dark days of the Nazi persecution in Europe. This is not an historical document. This is not an archive. It is a memoir, as accurate as I can make it, but it is dependent on my memories, and no one's memory is perfect.

The circumstances of my life in those days were harsh. The prolonged attacks on my sense of self came from many sources and were relentless. The profound loneliness and despair of those years was so painful that I choose to tell the story as succinctly as I can.

Ultimately, this book tells the story of a young girl's coming of age. It is about her spiritual journey to lift herself out of darkness and rise above pain and despair. It is about finding meaning and concentrating on the good in an evil world in order to become a whole person who is able to lead a constructive life.

In the course of my life, especially as a lecturer in high schools, I was exposed to attitudes and problems among young people from all walks of life. I would tell these children, especially those who have seen everything, that even if life puts you down and you have a rocky start, there is no reason to stay down. My peers and I, caught in that Nazi net, did not lack for excuses to fail. But we chose not to and learned that we all have the power to rise above terrible circumstances and make something positive of our lives.

This book is a success story. My story proves that each of us has the ability to transcend his fate. I started with one caring parent and one who was psychologically unstable, but they both instilled me with strong values that strengthened me mentally and physically and allowed me to survive. Along the way there were a few wonderful people who extended themselves to help me. I recognized them, and availed myself of their generosity of spirit. That was my choice. They opened the doors and the rest was up to me. My accomplishments came through hard work and much sacrifice. And I have achieved a fulfilling and productive life in America.

Sitting in my sunny office overlooking my garden, I reflect upon that life. Did I do enough for others? Did I do enough for myself? Could I have done more? When I was 25 years old, shortly after I came to America, Aunt Anny told me I had achieved enough. By that time I had worked my way through university—a dream come true—especially for a child whose formal education was a mess.

As memories flooded my mind, I decided I was blessed and realized that I had packed several lifetimes into one. I had abruptly changed the countries I lived in, the languages I spoke, and had to adapt to new cultures and social milieus. I received little or no help from anyone, except from a few wonderful people. There was no mentor to guide me. I learned through trial and error. My progress was slow, but I learned.

I earned a solid university education. I had a solid marriage and have three wonderful, accomplished children—all good and caring people, who make a positive contribution to society. I had two careers, one as a college professor for 14 years, and the other as a securities broker and Certified Financial Planner for 28 years.

Then I remember where I started—the road I took was long, arduous and uphill yet one I was determined to climb through war, persecution, prejudice, an unbalanced parent and the need to rely on charity. I yearned to lead a normal life, and once the war was over it took years, but I achieved my goals. The process of climbing out of that hole was slow, with many detours, before I learned to let go of hatred and see the creative energy and life force in every human being, before I was able to develop a life-affirming *Weltanschauung*, or world view, that liberated me.

In the immediate aftermath of the war I could not go dancing like other girls my age. I had to confront what had happened. As a teenager with no inner resources, I was compelled to face the horror in all its magnitude before I could go on. The role played by several teachers was crucial, as was my access to education. It allowed me to carry on an inner dialog with the best thinkers of the past, and by the time I earned my degree before coming to America, I was a whole person, a *mensch.*

Today, I enjoy the finer things in life—the arts, nature, friends and good times. I love to have fun, to dance and play. I have a tremendous curiosity about the world, a thirst for knowledge to help me understand how we got here and what makes us tick.

I am writing this book to inspire young people, to let them know things are never hopeless. They, too, can make the effort to work for a better life.

X

Table of Contents

In the Beginning

VIENNA
My Childhood and Early Memories

My name is Edith Mayer Cord, and I was born in Vienna between the wars. Vienna, the capital of Austria, looks as if its rococo and baroque buildings are giant wedding cakes. In the 19th century, the city of waltzes and Wiener schnitzel was practically considered the center of the universe, with the Austro-Hungarian Empire ruled by emperors and empresses. The First World War ended that!

When that earth-shattering war broke out, my parents were living with their families in Czernowitz, then part of the empire on the Russian border. In 1914, their families fled to Vienna to escape the Russian advance. At the time, there were two million residents in Vienna and 200,000 of them were Jews. My mother was 12, and her three older brothers were drafted to serve in the Austrian army as officers. The youngest one, Karl, was killed in 1916 in Italy, a loss from which my maternal grandmother, Rosa, and Mama never recovered.

My maternal grandfather, Josef Buchholz, was a sophisticated and handsome man with dark eyes and a stylish goatee. Though he had gotten his rabbinical ordination and could use the title, he didn't. He made his living as a wholesale food merchant, trading sardines by the wagonload, grain by the ton, chocolate and other foodstuffs by the box and barrel. Later, I learned that Jews had lived as merchants in Czernowitz for centuries, for the city was on a major trade route with access to the north, south, east and west.

Grandfather Josef Buchholz.
(Photo taken in Vienna.)

Growing up, Mama's family had servants and their standard of living was high. German was spoken at home and all the children attended German language schools and universities. My grandfather was a highly respected member of the community and the family had what is called *yichus*, Yiddish for status and ancestry.

On Papa's side of the family circumstances were modest. He was born in 1888 in Horodenka, also part of the old Austro-Hungarian Empire that later became part of Poland. His name was Schmil Juda, but everyone called him Adolf—in those days a popular name. (Two of my uncles later changed their names after the war because of Adolf Hitler, the Nazi leader).

When Papa was a year old, the family moved to Lemberg, renamed Lviv in what is now Ukraine. During Papa's boyhood, the family moved to Czernowitz and opened a clothing store. The families met when the Buchholzes patronized their store.

Papa, the oldest of eight children, often commented that he did not want to have many children—for then they raise themselves, and he wanted to raise us and retain control. As the oldest, he was very close to his father, and the *lingua franca* in their home was Yiddish.

Papa was short and stocky, with a round face, blue-gray eyes, very white skin, a high forehead and blond straight hair. As a child I noticed that the hair on his chest and on the back of his hands was black. He was clean shaven, except for a little stylish closely-trimmed moustache. He wore glasses and was losing his hair by the time I really got to know him in his forties.

Papa's father, Josef Mayer, had a limited command of German. When still a boy, my great-grandfather caught him trying to teach himself the Latin alphabet and ripped up the book. He said, *"Du wirst dech schmatten!"* ("[If you learn German] you will convert.") But yet my grandfather was literate in Hebrew and read the Yiddish newspaper. He made amends for what his father did to him by ensuring that Papa received an excellent secular education. Besides the required eight years of schooling, he sent Papa to a business academy for another four years. As a result, Papa had an excellent command of German and a solid general education.

After I was born, Papa took his 70-year-old parents to City Hall in order to have them married them under Austrian law. They were married according to Jewish law, but they never got a license because it was too expensive. Therefore, in the eyes of the Austrians, all children in unlicensed marriages were illegitimate and were assigned their mother's name. After the "wedding" he changed his name to Mayer,

Grandfather Josef Mayer.

Grandmother Rifka Ruchel Mayer, née Halpern.
(Photo taken in Vienna.)

My paternal grandparents in Karlsbad, 1925, holding their
little cup of mineral water. This photo on a postcard was sent
to my parents in Vienna. Written by my grandfather,
it is how I realized he could write German.

his father's surname. Papa's youngest brother, Oskar also changed his name to Mayer, but Michel remained a Halpern. It could be hard to explain, but some of my first cousins are Halperns, and my early papers call me Halpern, too.

Papa's concern was always to do things by the book, to adhere to the rule of law, and to acquire Austrian citizenship—as a former resident of a non-German speaking area he could choose between Austria and Romania. He proudly chose Austria, despite the fact that for reasons only the Austrians in their infinite wisdom could fathom Papa spent the years of the First World War in an Austrian detention camp as an "enemy alien." When he was released in 1918 he was 30 years old. Why Mama's brothers served in the Austrian army and Papa did not remains a mystery.

When the war ended, Mama's situation in Vienna became difficult. Her father decided to go back to Czernowitz, which had become part of Romania, to see whether anything was left of the family estate. He took his middle son, Leon, with him, and while there my grandfather died of a heart attack. Leon chose to stay in Czernowitz and married a woman named Klara. They had three children: Josef, Rosa and Karl.

During the Second World War that corner of Romania changed hands frequently. When the Soviets were in charge they drafted Leon's oldest son Josef. When the war was over, Josef ended up in the Soviet Union and was not allowed to leave. He married a Russian woman, had two daughters with her, worked somewhere as a foreman and ultimately was murdered by the Communists. The rest of the family managed to survive largely with the help of Karl.

After the war, my Uncle Leon and his wife tried to escape to Palestine with their daughter, Rosa. They were captured by the British and spent years in a detention camp in Cyprus until Israel was declared a state in 1948. Eventually Karl also escaped from the Communists and joined his family in Israel.

Mama was left in Vienna with her mother and her oldest brother Rudolf, who was in his early 30s. They were in the same apartment they lived in during the First World War. The apartment was on the fifth floor of a nice walk-up building in the first district—Werdertorgasse number 17, on the corner of the Franz Josef Kai near the Danube Canal.

The first district was a heavily Jewish neighborhood, though not as Jewish as the second district which had been given to Jews by King Leopold and was known as the Leopoldstadt. At the entrance to

My Austrian citizenship certificate dated August 9, 1934. It pictures the Rathaus, the beautiful city hall in Vienna. It was issued after Papa had his parents "married" under Austrian law, and reflects our name change from Halpern to Mayer.

the *Judengasse* was the *Judenplatz* where, Mama told me, they burned Jews in the Middle Ages. I remember thinking at the time: "I'm glad they don't do that any more." The fact remains that from early on I was aware that we were a persecuted minority, sort of second-class citizens. (Today they built a Holocaust memorial on that square.)

Mama was sent to a *pensionnat*, a private girls' school, until she was 16. Then, in 1919, Grandmother Rosa died of Spanish flu in the epidemic that killed millions, leaving Mama orphaned and destitute. She had a middle-class education, knew how to play the piano, spoke some French, and could embroider linens, but Mama had no marketable skills or money. The expensive life insurance policy my grandfather bought to protect her was paid, but the money was worthless because there was raging inflation in Austria.

From my mother's sad experience, as young as I was, I learned the importance of acquiring skills to support myself. I also learned to view the business of life insurance with a grain of salt, since we pay in good money and get back depreciated money, even with low inflation.

Rudolf and Mama's legal guardian (I never found out who he was) focused on finding Mama a husband. The story she told me was that a match (*shidduch*) was arranged with an older man who had money. She got engaged, but the engagement was broken by the groom, who gave her a substantial sum of money as a quit claim. As a result, Mama boasted that she was rich.

My parents met in Vienna between the wars, at a party given in honor of one of Papa's sisters on the eve of her wedding. Mama was just 17 or 18 years old. Papa was 32 and was being pressured by his family to take a wife. Though he was almost twice her age, he decided they should tie the knot. Papa would often tell us that he had been looking for Mama with a lantern, until he finally found her. Mama said only that she liked him, which was very different from the teenage crush she'd had on a distant cousin—and she made sure that my brother Kurt and I knew it!

After Grandmother Rosa died, Mama continued to live in the apartment with Rudolf, but when he got engaged, he wanted the apartment to himself. So to push the point, right after my parents were engaged, Rudolf locked Mama out of the apartment, forcing her to spend the night in the streets sitting with Papa on a park bench. Papa took Rudolf to court for his terrible act—which did not improve family relations—and the two couples were later forced to share the apartment.

My parents were married in November 1921. A year and a half later on March 10, 1923 my brother Kurt (Mordechai) was born. I

My father during his engagement.

My mother during her engagement.

came along in 1928, on the 15th of June, and yes, we all lived in that same place.

The apartment had its limitations. There was a cold-water faucet on the landing that served all the apartments on the floor. Inside there was a long hallway. To the left was a toilet. On the right was a door that led to two rooms occupied by Uncle Rudolf and his wife, who were later joined by their daughter Alice, nicknamed Lizzy. (Mama liked Lizzy, she said, because Lizzy looked like her. I had the opportunity to confirm the resemblance later in life when I met Lizzy as an adult. But in Vienna, we never spoke to each other, though we lived in the same apartment.)

Straight down the hall was another door leading to two more rooms occupied by my parents and, eventually, Kurt and me. Our windows opened to an inner courtyard, catty-cornered to my uncle's windows, so the families could hear everything going on in the other's living quarters.

I was only too well aware of the family discord throughout my childhood in Vienna, since their hatred for each other permeated the atmosphere.

When Mama became engaged to Papa, she'd given him her dowry. According to her, he spent it all setting his father up in a business. She resented that. In addition, Mama's relationship with Papa's family was a disaster. She despised all of them and had nothing good to say about any of them. On her wedding night, her mother-in-law wanted to check the sheets to see if she was a virgin—a custom in accordance with Jewish law—and Mama never forgave her for that. As for her in-laws, all but one were very well-to-do, and she was jealous.

As a result, we never socialized with my paternal aunts, uncles or cousins, or got invited to birthday parties, bar mitzvahs and other life-cycle events. Our only contact was through my grandparents or when Mama needed something. When we once visited an uncle's store, one of my aunts greeted us with, "What brings you here?" Mama took offense and never let it go. So when Mama kept telling me that I looked like Papa's sisters, it was not meant as a compliment—and I knew it.

According to Mama, after they married, Papa visited his parents every night, leaving her alone. She interpreted this as the result of his excessive devotion to his father. Initially I accepted Mama's view of things, but as a grown woman I wondered if Papa was happy with his young wife. He was 15 years her senior and an elegant dandy. Mama was an inexperienced young girl with a limited education and a sheltered upbringing.

My parents' wedding picture, Vienna, November 1921.

I also suspect that, at least, initially, my parents may have quarreled because, again according to Mama, Papa would say to her: "Do you want to quarrel like your parents did?" By the time I was old enough to understand, I never heard my parents quarrel. When once asked in school about my parents, I remember saying that they got along like two turtle doves.

Mama's friends were Finny Seider, younger sister to our next door neighbor, Frau Genia, and Dora Klapholz. They were inseparable and often called "*Das Drei Maederlhaus*" after a Viennese operetta about three girlfriends. When I was little, she had two other girlfriends she visited often. One was Frau Krochmal, who had a daughter one year older than I. We were playmates until she became sick and died.

Mama's other friend was a married woman with older children. She lived with her brother, a furrier, in the Leopoldstadt. Later, I heard her brother went back to Poland to find himself a wife.

Mama loved to talk, and when she ran into her friends on the street I would stand next to her, bored, anxious to leave, often tugging at her coat. I dreaded meeting Frau Dreif, one acquaintance who would pinch me hard on the cheek. She probably thought she was being cute or nice, but she hurt me, and I often wondered why Mama did not protect me from those pinches after I complained. One day Frau Dreif was heading in our direction, so I asked Mama to tell her not to pinch me. Mama did it while apologizing profusely for my rudeness.

Aside from our poverty, I would say that my parents had a solid marriage. Papa always treated Mama with respect, lifting his hat whenever he saw her coming down the street. In their marital relations they observed Jewish law, and she went to the ritual baths once a month. I had no idea what that meant, and even when I was old enough to learn about it, she never taught me a thing. When I was 18 and found a booklet about it on a laundry shelf, she ripped it out of my hand and said it wasn't for me.

I never saw them argue or heard them raise their voices. They had constant conversations. Papa always filled her in on his business dealings. Mama would sit and listen attentively, usually with some sewing or knitting in her hands. Subjects usually dealt with the political situation in Austria and Germany. Financial problems were a frequent topic, and Mama always pushed some idea or other for making money. When my parents did not want us to understand what they were talking about, they switched to Yiddish.

For her birthday, Papa often bought her books that he would read aloud to her while she did her handiwork. Occasionally, for a special

Kurt at age 3.

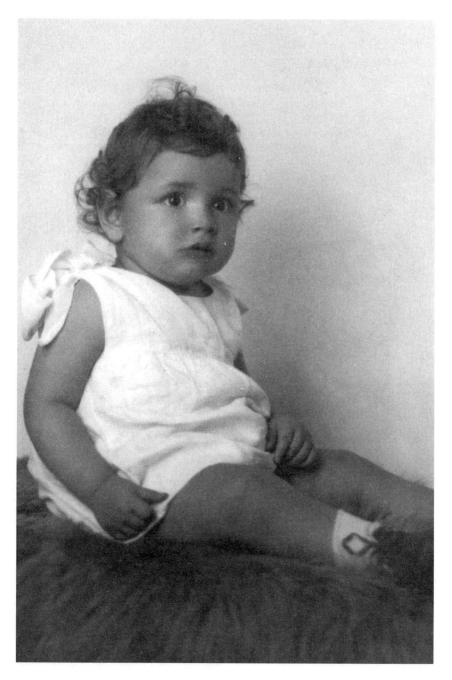

Me, age 1.

Papa with Kurt and me.
The caption reads: "Papa and our dear little children."

treat, they took us to the Yiddish theatre. I was as young as five or six and would usually fall asleep during the first act. When I could stay awake for the second act I felt proud of myself. I still remember Molly Picon in *Yidl mit dem Fiedl*. On the other hand, Papa did not like to go to the movies. So Mama went without him, usually dragging me along.

When I was born, Papa still owned a clothing store for men and boys on the Kaiserstrasse, a busy commercial street leading to a suburban railroad station. I remember going there as a little girl. Papa would give me a new *Janker*, one of those grey Tyrolian jackets with green lapels, whenever I outgrew the old one. I also remember getting a trench coat that was too big for me, but I grew into it.

After World War I that local railroad station was not used as much and eventually it was shut down, so there was less pedestrian traffic and less business for all the shops. The Depression did not help, either. Papa was forced to close his store, but refused to declare bankruptcy and insisted on paying off all his debts. My parents had a small metal lockbox where they kept their cash, and every so often Mama took some money to buy food until it was all gone. I wore hand-me-downs from my cousins, and I remember standing on a chair and crying, when I was two or three, because my mother had me try on scratchy woolen sweaters they'd given us.

On Saturday afternoons we often visited my paternal grandparents. They would put peanuts on the large dining room table for us to munch and served us tea with lemon and sugar in glasses set in silver holders. The children sat around the table while the grownups talked in another room. I often played a board game with my cousin, Erich Katz, who was my age.

When I was about 3, Mama had surgery for an ectopic pregnancy, and I was sent to stay with my paternal grandparents for six weeks. My grandfather was blinded as a result of a streetcar accident just before I was born, and while I stayed with them, I would sit on a low stool next to him and act as his eyes. I would take him by the hand, lead him wherever he wanted to go and open doors for him.

My grandmother told my parents that I was no trouble, except that I was a very slow eater. Since chubby babies were considered healthy babies, in those days they stuffed me with lots of cream of wheat. My only defense was to eat very slowly. They treated me well and gave me a doll, but there were no children for me to play with, and the little stool was the only place for me to sit because it was the only chair in the house that was my size.

Before I was old enough to go to school, Mama would take me shopping to the Karmelitermarkt for produce. When it snowed, Mama took the sled and pulled me along, storing the groceries between my legs. In the fall we would walk through the Kaipark, the park along the Danube Canal. (It no longer exists and has been replaced by a highway.) I would be allowed to gather horse chestnuts to take home for arts and crafts projects. (I would make holes in them and string them up to make a chain.)

It was always a treat when, in nice weather, Mama would take me to the park, mostly on Saturday afternoons. There was a circle of gravel and grass called a Rondo, with benches around it, in the center of the park. There was no playground, because in those days they didn't exist outside of private pre-schools. I could jump rope or play with my Diabolo, a rubber spool that spins on a string connected to two sticks. When it gathered speed, you would toss it in the air and catch it on the string like Chinese jugglers do. It took some practice but I became very good at it.

Like Victorian children, I also had a hoop with a stick. I very much wanted a Triton scooter but it remained an unfulfilled wish. I also remember standing at the fence enclosing the ice skating rink, my face pressed against the cold metal, watching longingly as skaters twirled to the "Skaters' Waltz."

There were always children in the park, but I did not know them because I went there so rarely. I was too shy to speak to them or join in their play, so I mostly remained an outsider and watched. One incident stands out in my mind. I must have been four, and was at the park with Mama on one of our rare outings. The other children were playing a game—something like musical chairs, but using trees. They sang a silly nursery rhyme, *Vater, Vater, Leih mir d'Scher, wo ist leer?* ("Father, Father, lend me your scissors, where is it empty?") You had to leave your tree and get to another before you were tagged. I was so happy to be included in the game that, when nature called, I refused to leave for fear of losing my place—and ended up wetting my pants, a most embarrassing situation.

Papa was the bright spot in my life. Papa was a charming fellow, playful, funny, and outgoing. He was a master storyteller and I often told him that he was in the wrong profession: He should have been a poet instead of a businessman. Little did I realize that poets have a tough time making a living. He played the violin by ear and, when he came back from his trips to Italy, would play Italian songs for us. He also loved to play cards and he and Mama played gin rummy with their friends.

Papa in Vienna.

Mama in Vienna, age 34.
(Photo taken in 1937.)

Papa had a tuning fork that he would strike against a hard object and then put to my ear so that I could listen to it hum. Music was an important part of his life and he transferred that love to me. We had a radio that played Viennese waltzes, arias from operettas, Hungarian music, Brahms, Liszt and other popular classical music. When Papa came home at the end of the day, he would shout, "How can you live without music?" and turn on the radio. But when Papa's taxes went unpaid, the tax collector would come to the apartment to collect the only thing left of value: the radio. Our other valuables—like the silver candlesticks—were already in the pawn shop. Whenever some money came in, Papa would run to retrieve the radio.

I loved to sing and loved music as much as Papa did, but there was no money for music lessons. I knew my cousins were taking dancing lessons, because they showed me photographs of themselves in ballerina dresses. I wanted to be a ballerina and dance, too.

Mostly I dreamed of owning my very own teddy bear. Whenever we went to visit Frau Genia next door, I was allowed to play with a brown teddy bear and was always sad when I had to go home and leave it behind. Then, when I was seven, I developed a sore throat with high fever. Mama could not take me to the market and had to leave me home alone, so she asked me to stay in bed while she went shopping. She came back with a big box for me. My eyes popped wide open when I opened it and found a teddy bear with golden yellow hair, stuffed with straw inside. It had a black nose and glass eyes. I kept that teddy bear throughout our years of wandering. After I married and had Emily, I gave her my precious bear. She played with it until it fell apart, but by then I was ready to let it go.

Papa was a heavy smoker and suffered from nicotine poisoning. We knew smoking was bad for him, so Kurt and I would encourage him to throw away his half-smoked cigarette. After cutting down initially, he resumed his habit—and had another bout of nicotine poisoning. Kurt and I badgered him not to smoke but to no avail—until the third episode, which made him very sick. We all stood around his bed with the doctor, who pleaded with him to stop smoking: "You have a wife and young children...." That day Papa quit cold turkey. I believe that Kurt and I were "vaccinated" against smoking, because we witnessed my father's struggle with nicotine addiction.

Kurt and I vied for his attention and Papa would often play with each one of us in turn. During the first six years of my life he spent time with me. He taught me games—cards, checkers, chess—and told me stories. I had a choice between grandfather stories, Sherlock Holmes stories—he was a Sherlock Holmes fan—and Bible stories. Much of my knowledge of the Bible came from his bedtime stories.

Judaism was an important part of our lives. Papa was very religious, putting on *tallis* and *tefillin* (prayer shawl and phylacteries) every morning. My parents kept a kosher home and observed the Sabbath and holidays. Every Friday night the table was set with a white cloth and candles, even when the fare was meager. Still, Mama usually managed to buy a carp for *Shabbat*. We would go down to the Danube Canal and pick out a fish from the holding tank. The fishwife would then kill it with a blow to the head, remove the scales and clean out the insides. Mama would then prepare it for our dinner. Chicken was a rare treat and reserved for holidays.

In spite of the importance my parents attached to religion, my religious education was mediocre. My parents hired a tutor, Mr. Ringel—who was even poorer than we were—who taught me the Hebrew alphabet. The Bible story he delighted in telling me over and over was the story of Adam and Eve, and how Eve was the one who had tempted Adam to disobey God. Needless to say I did not learn much.

Kurt and I attended the Seitenstettentempel, the main synagogue on the Seitenstettengasse, where there was a one-hour youth service on Saturday afternoons. Papa went to a little *shul* (synagogue) in the Judengasse where he would spend Friday nights, Saturday mornings and often Saturday afternoons until *Shabbat* was over and marked with the *Havdalah* ceremony. Many times I would meet him there in the afternoon and stayed with him until *Havdalah*, since it was a good excuse to get out of the house. The old men there would always fuss over me.

On Sundays Papa usually took us to museums: the Kunsthistorische Museum and the Naturhistorische Museum. Mama never went along because I guess it was her day off. As I've already noted, Mama loved going to the movies, but Papa didn't. I think that, for her, the movies were an escape. When she could spare a schilling she would take me with her. I saw some of Rudolf Valentino's silent films and *Ben Hur*. She told me I should know the classics. I also saw new films as they came out, but I confess the kissing scenes bored me no end

As a special treat on birthdays, Papa would take us to the Prater, the big Viennese amusement park. Though we couldn't afford the rides, I do have a picture of him holding me on a papermaché horse, taken at a photographer's booth. The photo is inscribed: "For my little daughter on her sixth birthday," and I look happy.

Papa and me at the Prater. The caption reads: As a souvenir of our
outing to the Prater on June 17, 1934. Papa and his little daughter
Edith Halpern on her 6th birthday June 15, 1934.

When I was 4 years old, Mama sent me to a Montessori kindergarten. I caught everybody's germs and my colds were very severe. I was always treated with warm milk, butter and honey, a concoction I hated, and given inhalants that I also hated.

In preschool I was painfully shy, unused to being with other children. As a consequence, I could not stand up for myself. Because of that and my absences, Mama took me out of school. The following year she signed me up again. I was 5 years old but still had trouble standing up for myself. My report card said I was very sensitive, so they placed me with the 4-year-olds.

In wintertime, cold was a constant companion. Viennese winters are harsh, with lots of snow crackling underfoot. The apartment, too, was always cold. We had a floor-to-ceiling green tile oven facing into both rooms and Mama built a fire every morning. During the night the fire would die, and by morning the apartment was freezing. Until Mama built a fresh fire and the place warmed up, I would sit on my little stool, freezing, with my hands in my pockets, shoulders hunched. There were no snowsuits for children back then, and I wore thin cotton stockings and hand-me-down shoes with holes in the soles. Mama would stuff newspaper into the shoes, which would get wet in rainy and snowy weather. As a result, I often sat in school with cold, wet feet.

I remember the school well. It was a stimulating environment with many things to do. I was allowed to do things that had been forbidden at home, like using scissors. I was taught to tie my shoelaces, something I loved because it made me independent. Before that I always had to plead with Mama to tie my shoelaces. It was a huge task for me, because Mama insisted that I wear laced ankle boots until I was eight years old. She said it would strengthen my ankles, but the opposite is true. As I grew older I often twisted my ankles because they were too weak to hold me.

School was a world apart, and gave me great joy. I loved the small furniture in our classroom that felt custom-fit for me. I got along well with the children and related well to the teachers. I frequently volunteered to help serve lunch. The volunteers had to eat first and finish their spinach, so I ate my spinach. Then I was allowed to push the serving cart while a teacher ladled out the soup and served the food.

My parents enrolled me in the Boerseschule in the Boersegasse, for first grade, not far from where we lived. Mama always walked me to school and picked me up because, she said, she was afraid gypsies might snatch me away. By the time I was in third grade most children went to school by themselves, but Mama insisted on being my chaperone. By then I was chafing at the bit and wanted to be like the other children—independent enough to walk to school on my own.

There were about 40 children in each class. Students came from all social classes, and there were even a few Jewish girls from wealthy families, but I did not socialize with them. I was keenly aware that they were always well-dressed and hung out with each other.

Two children shared each desk, which was fixed to the floor. When we weren't writing, we had to sit up straight with our arms crossed, or with our hands folded on top of the desk. Sometimes the teachers ordered us to sit with our arms crossed behind our backs.

Despite my social isolation, I did very well. The grading system went by numbers—five was the lowest grade, equivalent to an F, and one was the equivalent of an A. I rated an occasional two in gym, sewing or drawing and earned ones in all my academic subjects. "*Lauter Einser wie die Soldaten*" my grandmother would say when she saw my grades ("All ones lined up like soldiers.") My parents never praised me for my scholastic accomplishments because they took them for granted. Maybe they didn't want to compliment me because they thought I'd get a swelled head.

The students were divided into three sections: A, B and C. Section A was for the best students and C for the weakest. Classes went from 9 A.M. to 12 noon, Monday through Saturday, and we were given an hour of homework daily. The Saturday compromise approved by the school because of our family's religious observance was that I would go to class but would not write on Saturdays.

My teachers were older women—my first grade teacher retired at the end of that year—who ran no-nonsense classrooms. We learned a lot from them. With only three grades in elementary school under my belt before we left Vienna, I was able to read fluently and write German without mistakes. I practiced my penmanship and covered pages with each letter of the alphabet, learning capitals and Latin script. We also studied *Fraktur* or Gothic script that was heavily used at the time.

Though just out of third grade, I had already memorized the multiplication table and mastered long division. To this day I count in German. The only time Papa helped me with homework was when I had to memorize the alphabet in first grade, and he made up a song for me. He also helped me memorize the multiplication tables. Otherwise, I was on my own—except for walking to and from school.

We learned about Austrian history and World War I. While still in Vienna I read *The Prince and the Pauper* by Mark Twain in German translation. I read *Altneuland* by Theodore Herzl about his dream of a Jewish state and *Das Volk des Ghetto* (*The People of the Ghetto*), a compilation of stories with mystical overtones. I read *Little Lord Fauntleroy* and tried *Uncle Tom's Cabin* but could not finish it because it was so sad and made me cry. Of course I read most of *Grimm's Fairy Tales* where the good are always rewarded and the bad punished. Early on I learned to admire Schiller and, of course, Goethe. Two poems by Schiller stand out. One about the forging of a bell, "Die Glocke," celebrated the virtue of work. The other, "Die Buergschaft," was a powerful poem about friendship and loyalty. Another book I found enchanting and exotic was *A Thousand and One Arabian Nights*.

I had few books, so I read my favorites as many as eight times over. I skipped over the theoretical passages in Herzl, where he described his vision of a Jewish state. I was more interested in the story. As for Mark Twain, the story fascinated me, but there, too, I skipped over the lengthy and to me sometimes boring descriptions of pageantry. I didn't understand his biting social commentary until much later.

When I was 4, Papa's father died. Papa then decided to go into a new wholesale business. A year later, an apartment became available in my grandmother's building, Seitenstettengasse 5. It was a large apartment with three rooms and a kitchen that had running water. There was a toilet in the apartment but it was not heated, so going to the bathroom during the winter was an unpleasant experience. I always dreaded it and would put it off as long as I could. There was no hallway either. It was a railroad apartment. On the day of the move Kurt and I ran around the apartment in circles, pushing my doll carriage. I was 5 years old, Kurt was 10.

The apartment excited Mama with its potential. I can still see Mama in her nightgown, walking around and talking with Papa about her design plans. As I watched them, I vividly remember thinking that these were pipe dreams and, young as I was, I was right!

Papa put shelves and a phone in the largest room and bought dry goods to sell, but somehow the business did not take off. My Uncle Michel had a successful clothing store, so did the two brothers Katz who had married Papa's sisters. Their store was on one of the major shopping streets, Mariahilferstrasse. His youngest brother, Uncle Oskar, also had a successful store—but no one in the family did business with

Papa. It must have been humiliating for him, and Papa complained about it to Mama.

The fact remains that although Papa could not make a living in Vienna he wouldn't leave the city as long as his parents were alive. When our financial situation deteriorated, perhaps the wealthier siblings paid for our groceries because their mother ordered them to do that. They never gave us money, but Mama charged food in a dairy store and they paid for it. While I did not go to bed hungry, my diet lacked meat, fruits and vegetables, consisting mostly of hot cereal, bread, butter, milk and eggs. I developed eczema on the back of my knees from a vitamin deficiency. After that, Mama always made an effort to feed me the proverbial apple a day.

There were few family outings. During the summer months we rarely visited the Stadion, a large park with swimming pools, even though summers in Vienna could be oppressively hot. I vaguely remember a couple of excursions to the Kahlenberg just outside of Vienna and to Schoenbrunn and the Belvedere. But those trips may have been taken with Papa, not as a family.

We went on vacation twice during the nine years I spent in Vienna. The first time was after Kurt's appendectomy, when he was ten and I was five. He needed fresh air to help him recover from a protracted convalescence. We rented a room at a working farm and Kurt had a wonderful time. The farmer let him climb on the horse-drawn cart and hold the reins. There were farm animals and constant activity. I saw a chicken being killed when the farmer twisted its neck and then, to my amazement, I saw the chicken run around without its head. The image stayed with me and convinced me that killing an animal according to Jewish law was more merciful.

Kurt fell in love with the place and, later, during the Second World War, while we were in hiding in the French village of Montlaur, he said he would go to Canada when it was over and become a farmer. He said farmers never go hungry.

The second vacation was about a year later. I had been diagnosed with tuberculosis and my parents were advised to take me to heal in the fresh air. We went to the Burgenland, a rural area not far from Vienna, where my parents rented a cottage near a stream. I have often drawn pictures of the place. Though there was not much to do there, it was a welcome change of pace from Vienna. We often hiked to the nearest village, up a steep path lined with blackberry bushes. Kurt would gather berries and, once, while leaning too far to get to the riper berries, he fell into the bushes, was scratched by the thorns and got up covered

Kurt and I in Vienna, I'm 5 and Kurt is 10.

with blood,. Once we made it to the village, to the innkeeper's surprise, Mama ordered a glass of Schnapps. She used it to disinfect my brother's "wounds." Later, the innkeeper came over to tell us he didn't think Mama was going to drink it.

These two vacations were paid for by relatives. When Kurt had to recuperate, Mama went to her wealthy cousin, Anna Freudenheim, our *Tante* (Aunt) Anna, to ask her for the money. I don't know who paid for the second vacation.

Tante Anna was my mother's first cousin on her mother's side. She was married to Adolf (who later changed his name to Alfred) Freudenheim. He was an executive, possibly even the CEO of the Montan Union, the Austrian affiliate of Standard Oil. They had no children. He had a sister, Klara Wachstein, who was divorced. Klara had lost her older child, a boy, to meningitis. She also had a daughter, Paula. Klara and Paula lived with the Freudenheims, who treated the little girl as if she were their own. Paula married an engineer and went to live in Poland. They were killed during the Holocaust.

I loved visiting *Tante* Anna. She lived on the Schwarzenbergplatz in a very large apartment with nine or 10 rooms. There was a *Herrenzimmer*, a library with dark paneling to which the men withdrew to smoke their cigars, drink brandy and discuss business and politics. There was also a formal drawing room, or salon, and a sitting room where we stayed whenever we visited. The place was comfortable and cozy, and nice and warm in winter.

Kurt and I were always served a tasty snack and then it was time to play with Paula while the grown-ups talked. I thought Paula had such interesting games. While tiddly-winks is commonplace today, in those days I thought it was the greatest.

Paula was older than I and I admired her tremendously. She seemed to have everything I could only dream of: a comfortable home, nice clothes, good food, dancing lessons, horseback riding lessons and vacations. I thought she was very pretty with her dark eyes, black wavy hair, sensitive features and tall, slender figure. She was always nice to us.

The only bad thing about our visits was in the wintertime, when we had to take the long, freezing walk home through the Stadtpark, past the Johann Strauss monument. Streetcars were just too expensive. How I remember those walks!

On rare occasions *Tante* Anna would visit us in the Werdertorgasse, and would always bring me a bar of milk chocolate. She was a tall,

Anna Buchholz (my mother), age 17, and Anna Berler (my Aunt Anny) and her future husband, Adolf (Alfred) Freudenheim, ca. 1920.

stately woman, always dressed in good taste, with rounded, attractive features. I remember her long legs, covered in silk stockings. It would be 15 years before I would see her again in New York—where she became Aunt Anny.

Aunt Anny made it to New York after the *Anschluss* (the German annexation of Austria). She and Alfred fled Vienna for Paris where Alfred continued to work for a subsidiary of Standard Oil. When France fell in 1940, they escaped to Lisbon and boarded the last ship for Cuba. There they waited for their quota for two years until they were able to immigrate to the United States. Alfred developed an export-import business with an office on Wall Street. Aunt Anny remained a beautiful, elegant woman to the end.

For Mama in Vienna, housework was a full-time job. We had no maid, so Mama did all the wash by hand and had to shop and cook food daily because there was no place to keep it fresh—we had no ice box. Water had to be carried into the apartment from the landing. Life was really hard for her.

My parents were strict disciplinarians and demanded respect from Kurt and me. We were required to address them in the third person, as if they were royalty. We also used "kiss the hand" as our greeting to them, and I even had to curtsy to my grandmother. My parents wanted us to believe that only they knew everything and that they were perfect. I recall how shocked I was when, at 15, after I had left home, how far from perfect they were. In the end, their attitude toward child-rearing prevented Kurt and me from developing our own judgments and street smarts.

Mama's idea of discipline was harsh corporal punishment. She would pull down my panties and spank my bare bottom. Since that hurt her hand, she began hitting me with a wicker rug beater. When I got older, she would slap me across the face. I hated that and recall clearly that I could not wait to grow up so that she could not beat me anymore.

Kurt and I often squabbled when I was little. But when he became a teenager we had less interaction. He had a life of his own and I spent all my free time with Mama. It wasn't until we fled to France during the war, when I was 13 and he was 18 that I felt strongly connected to him. He was tall and, I thought, handsome. I was very proud to be seen with him. Unfortunately, this was not to last.

Looking back, I would say that Mama did not encourage much interaction between us. It seemed as though everything had to go through her as if she were the center and we were the spokes of a wheel. Perhaps it was her way of retaining control over both of us. In fact, I would say that both my parents wanted to retain total control over us no matter how old we were.

Kurt was generally as obedient as I was, but sometime around his bar mitzvah there was trouble. After four years of elementary school, Kurt was enrolled in the *Realgymnasium*, an academically-oriented secondary school. He took Latin and needed a tutor who maintained that Kurt was capable of doing the work on his own but needed a tutor to make sure he did it. Something was awry.

I was vaguely aware that my parents sought professional advice and were told to sign Kurt up with a youth organization so that he could be with his peers. He joined Betar, the Josef Trumpeldor Zionist organization. It was one of the happiest experiences of his life. He went to meetings, made lots of friends and, in the summertime, went to a camp in the Salzkammergut by the Wolfgangsee.

To make that possible, Mama went to *Tante* Anna and begged for money. Fritzi, Frau Genia's daughter who was a year older than Kurt, was allowed to join him in the summer camp. While there, Kurt fell in love with an athletic looking young girl in pigtails and photographed her with the camera he had received for his bar mitzvah. In the camp picture he looks radiant and happy.

Though Papa often threatened to spank my brother—he never touched me—he gave Kurt a beating only once, when we lived in Italy. Papa was very angry because Kurt, at age 14 or 15, refused to go to services on Saturday morning. Kurt had started his Hebrew education at the age of 4. I started at age 6, but since my Jewish education was not taken seriously I never became fluent in Hebrew, Mr. Ringel notwithstanding.

Mama always yelled at Kurt and me and frequently used sarcasm. She blamed me for everything. On Mother's Day, when I was 7 years old, I promised myself to do everything I could to please her. But by 10 A.M. she was already yelling. In fact, I was almost 50 years old before I stopped trying to please her.

Mama knew she had a problem, but instead of doing something about it she'd say, "I'm nervous. That's how I am." She didn't consider her lack of self-control a shortcoming and never tried self-improvement. But she knew enough never to yell at Papa and was on her best behavior when he was around. Kurt and I were her victims when no one was looking. She didn't stop her violence even when we were teenagers. One day Kurt was big enough and strong enough to stop her. When

Kurt, the bar mitzvah boy, in Vienna, 1936. He received a Kodak
camera for his bar mitzvah. After that we always had pictures. He
loved his camera, a hobby I inherited from him.

Kurt's Betar summer camp. He is standing, second from left.
Fritzi is next to him, third from left.

(l-r) Fritzi and Frau Genia in the Stadtpark, Vienna, 1937.

she started hitting him, he grabbed her arms near the wrist and held them away from his body. That infuriated her even more.

As a result of all of this trauma, the Germanic emphasis on obedience and a strict religious upbringing, I was cowed into submission and very shy. When Papa was away, every letter he sent ordered me to obey Mama. Things didn't get better as I got older. After the Holocaust, in Toulouse, she would often tell me I was crazy. All this made it hard for me to become a whole person with a modicum of self-confidence. I know Mama used to brag about me behind my back, but my relationship with her was painful.

Mama also told me I was an "accident," but I think I was a "wanted accident." While that sounds like an oxymoron, it isn't. On the one hand my parents did not feel they could afford another child, yet emotionally they were ready to have one. Anyway, there I was and Papa seemed very happy to have a little girl. He was a loving and entertaining companion and I have warm memories of my childhood with him.

Mama took care of us, but she never played with us. Her life was never easy and she had lots of difficulty coping with her children and her circumstances. She tried to treat Kurt and me equally. If she bought me something nice to eat, *einen Leckerbissen*, she would bring Kurt something too. One thing I disliked intensely was getting Kurt's discarded school supplies. I never had the pleasure of experiencing the sweet smell of a brand new eraser, the smooth feel of a full-length pencil that hadn't yet been chewed and its woodsy scent, or using new pen nibs that hadn't already been broken in. I would dream of clutching a brand new eraser in my hand, only to wake up and find an empty palm.

Despite her transparent attempts at equal treatment, it was clear to me that she favored my brother. He was her firstborn, a boy and, most important, she said he looked like her side of the family. Mama's dislike of Papa's sisters was known to me, and when she constantly told me that I looked just like them, I got the message. She praised Kurt for being a good eater, and denigrated me for eating like a little girl.

Perhaps this was a result of her emotional childhood traumas. When my grandmother was pregnant with Mama, she was very unhappy about it, and she told her the cold, cruel facts when Mama was still a child. My grandmother had three sons and did not want another child. She even told Mama she tried to cause a miscarriage, but it didn't work. Since Mama was a girl, my grandmother reconciled herself to Mama's existence, though my grandfather was very pleased. The only picture I have of Mama as a child was taken when she was about 6 years old, soon after she recovered from typhoid fever. She looks scrawny and pale as she stands next to her mother—a tall, overweight, but elegantly dressed matron. Mama's large brown eyes look straight at the camera and she is not smiling.

Her brothers abused her and called her *das Traskobjekt* (the punching bag). As a result, she never allowed Kurt to hit me, though she more than made up for that herself. Her youngest brother, Karl, was the only one who paid attention to her. He helped her with schoolwork, and often made her copy entire pages out of books.

She would describe how her large family gathered around a generously laden dining room table and how relatives would visit. She would always end her stories with *"Es war schoen"* ("It was beautiful"). While her father was probably nice to her, I have the feeling he was distant. The only one she would talk about was Karl, whose photographs and student mementos she kept and treasured to the end of her life. When he was killed in Italy, she became emotionally crippled.

I was 6 years old when Papa's mother died. Now Papa decided to leave Vienna to seek his fortune. A Mr. Hirschkrohn manufactured leather jackets and raincoats in Vienna and agreed to fund Papa's expenses as his salesman in Italy. And so Papa left for Italy, even though he couldn't speak Italian. He was gone for weeks and months at a time. When traveling in Italy he continued to eat kosher food by sticking to dairy restaurants called *latterias* and he always carried his *tallis* and *tefillin* with him in his briefcase.

When he came back to Vienna, he spent more time with his supplier and with Mama, but not with Kurt and me.

The family saw very little of him during those three years, and we still had little money. To make ends meet, Mama rented out two of our three rooms. Two ladies inhabited the large room in the front and an ultra-Orthodox young couple lived in the back room off the kitchen. We kept the middle room for ourselves, meaning we had to walk through the room rented to the two women in order to get to ours. To avoid disturbing them, we stayed in our own room as much as possible, and in the evenings felt like prisoners in our own home. Mama used the rent money to buy produce and occasionally hamburger meat, chicken or carp.

By 1936 Papa was becoming successful and was unhappy about the long separations from the family. He decided to move us to Genoa

Grandmother Rosa Buchholz, née Berler, with Mama, age 6.
Mama was recovering from typhoid fever.

the following year. My parents waited for Kurt to finish his fourth and final year in the *Gymnasium.*

My parents were also watching the rise of Nazism in Germany and in Austria with much anxiety, so the decision seemed a wise one. Mama had a year to sell off the furniture, store some things with friends and get the family ready for the big move.

I don't understand the contrast between my parents' political sophistication and their naïveté. I remember their talks about the rise of Nazism, the mention of the *Voelkischer Beobachter* and *Der Stuermer* (two Nazi newspapers), the signing of the Concordat with the Vatican's Cardinal Pacelli, later Pope Pius XII, and the shooting of Chancellor Dollfuss, who was forced to bleed to death because Nazi guards posted at his bedside would not let a doctor near him. My parents read Swiss newspapers, *Die Basler Nachrichten, Die Neue Zuericher Zeitung* and, more regularly, *Die Weltwoche* because these papers were objective. They were well informed. But what did Papa do? He wanted Austrian citizenship! And I remember how happy he was when we finally got those papers. How ironic! With Romanian papers we would have had a better chance of surviving.

I don't recall saying goodbye to family or friends except for Frau Genia, her daughter Fritzi and her old father, Mr. Seider. Papa came to Vienna to pick us up. Most of our stuff had been shipped ahead, so we carried just a few suitcases to the station. This was my first major travel adventure; I still remember the train ride across the Brenner Pass. I was singing a song I had learned in school: "*O ade du mein lieb' Heimatland* ("Goodbye my sweet fatherland")... "*Da gruess ich dich zum letzen Mal*" ("Here I greet you for the last time").

Little did I know that I was lucky to be leaving. I was not sad. Papa was with us and I felt we were going to a better life.

I was just 9 years old.

My first grade classroom. I'm in the second row on the right.

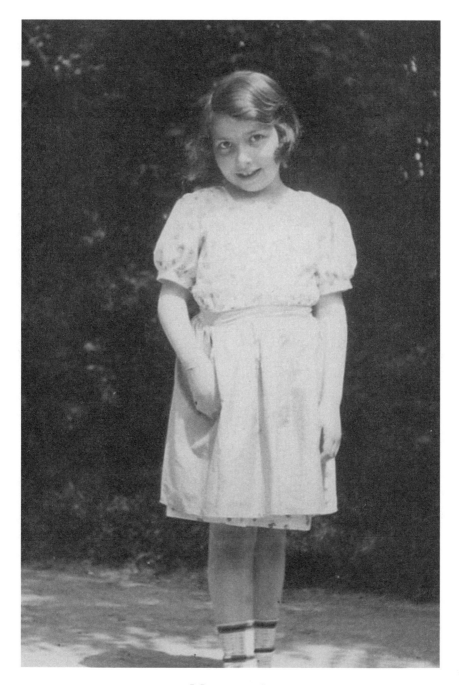

Me at age 8.

Mama and I in Vienna, 1937. I am 9 years old.

GENOA
The Happiest Year of My Life

It must have been late August or September 1937 when we left Vienna for Italy. Leaving the familiar for the unknown, I had mixed feelings. But when we went through the Brenner Pass, where the train was stopped for at least two hours as we were checked by customs officers, our mood was upbeat. We were looking forward to a better life as a family.

We disembarked in Venice. It was exciting to be in a city built on water. Kurt and I immediately wanted to go for a ride in a gondola, but Mama was afraid of the water and thought the gondola was unstable, so we contented ourselves with the *vaporetti*, little steam powered ferries that shuttle passengers along the myriad canals. (Today the ferries are motor driven, but they are still called *vaporetti*.) We were in Venice for only two days, but it was long enough for me to fall in love with the city—and I've been back many times since.

Then it was off to Genoa. When we got there, I was the beneficiary of a luxury I had never known. Papa rented a furnished apartment and for the first time in my life I had my own bedroom. I was happy to have my own space, but on the first night Mama's worst fears were confirmed. In Vienna she had put chairs at the side of my youth bed to prevent me from falling out. Though here the bed was higher, she chose not to do so. Of course that first night I fell out of bed, hit my forehead and scraped off enough skin to leave me with a scar for quite some time.

We lived in that apartment for about six weeks, until my parents bought a co-op on the Via Zara, a nice street with lovely villas and a few high-rise apartment buildings, not far from the new sports stadium.

My parents bought new furniture and Mama happily stayed home. She finally had enough money to indulge her passion for cooking and baking to her heart's content.

I can still see her in the kitchen, her lower arms bare, sprinkling flour on a white tablecloth. When making apple strudel, she stretched the dough over the tablecloth until it was paper thin and yet never broke. She spread the dough with apples, raisins, cinnamon and sugar, then grabbed one end of the tablecloth and rolled the filled dough on itself until she had a long strudel she shaped into a horseshoe and carefully placed in a baking pan. I was allowed to watch, but not touch or even help.

Kurt wasn't interested in going back to school, so Papa, through his business contacts, found him a job in Produzione Industrie Tesseli, a haberdashery in the Galleria Mazzini.

The store was run by three handsome Italian brothers who still lived with their parents. All three were single and all three had mistresses. Of course, this immorality greatly displeased Mama. She was terrified that the brothers would exert a bad influence on Kurt. But Kurt was earning good pocket money while learning a trade and he was happy. The brothers took him under their wing, and sometimes invited him to their parents' house. He liked going there and always commented on the luxurious three egg omelets they served. Kurt was always ravenous and often bought sandwiches at the automat between meals.

Kurt kept in touch with his friends from Vienna by mail, but Mama invaded his privacy, read his mail and criticized what she read. Before long, he told his friends to write to him care of general delivery and that was something I did later, for the same reason.

I was continuing my education. Papa signed me up at the small Sephardic Jewish day school. The Sephardic community was very old and well established. Classes were held on the top floor of the new triple-domed Sephardic temple. The sanctuary was very impressive and the school modern. Our desks and chairs could be moved around and, at first, I thought that was disorderly compared to our fixed desks in Vienna. It didn't take long before I adjusted to the freedom of movement.

After three years of elementary school in Vienna, I could read and write German. In Genoa, I didn't yet speak Italian, so they put me back in third grade. The teacher was young, quite a contrast to my elderly Viennese teachers. She was lively and pleasant and tried her best to help me learn the language. I caught on quickly and by the end of the year I was fluent in Italian.

Kurt's employers: the father and the three sons. (Mario is in the front, on the right). Genoa, February 14, 1939.

We continued to speak German at home and I read literature in German. Mama brought along Kurt's textbooks, including the readers. So before I could read *Pinocchio* in Italian, I read the *Nibelungenlied*, a medieval saga that was the basis of Wagner's Ring Cycle. The reading helped me maintain, and even strengthened, my knowledge of German.

My history lessons were very interesting. In Vienna, when we studied World War I, we learned that the Austrians and Germans were in the right, the French and British were the primary bad guys, and the Italians were a close second. In Italian history class, the Italians were the good guys, the French and the English were okay, and the Germans and the Austrians were the bad guys. Consequently, by the time I was 9, I learned not to trust the printed word. Later, when studying in France, I got the French version which only confirmed my skepticism.

The school was quite a distance from home, so I was picked up by a limousine that had been converted into a school bus. I thought being chauffeured to and from school was the height of luxury and I was in seventh heaven. Another new experience was making lots of friends and being invited to birthday parties and other outings.

I was also much more at ease in a Jewish school. In Vienna, during the Christmas season, we sang carols in school, something that made me uncomfortable. Also adding to my discomfiture was my attendance problem: I had to be absent on Jewish holidays yet went to school on *Shabbat*. In Genoa, I could sing Chanukah songs instead of Christmas carols and there were no classes on *Shabbat* or Jewish holidays. The teachers would even produce an elaborate Purim play with the students.

Better yet, Genoa was sunny and warm, with bright blue skies. Gone were the harsh Viennese winters. I loved the way the city looked, too. With a narrow level coastline at the foot of the Alps, most of Genoa is built on foothills that drop into the Tyrrhenian Sea. The hilly part of the city looked like children's blocks thrown helter-skelter against the hillside. There were gleaming villas with pastel colored stucco exteriors looking down at us. In the sunset the hills took on a golden glow. It was beautiful.

Papa was around most of the time. While he did not spend as much time with me as he had in Vienna, I did not miss him because I was busy with school, the challenge of learning Italian and my budding social life. It was the happiest year of my childhood.

Mama did not do as well. Although Papa was there and she had money, she missed her friends in Vienna. In the spring she had a

The beautiful Sephardic synagogue in Genoa.
The Jewish day school was on the top floor.

gallbladder attack and was quite ill. With small changes in her diet she did well, though she still complained.

Each apartment in our building came with patio space on the roof. Ours was the size of a large room and we used it to hang our laundry out to dry. Most of our neighbors did the same thing. A few people turned their spaces into little gardens or outdoor rooms. It was all pleasant, and felt very safe. One night Mussolini came to the nearby stadium to deliver a speech. We all went up to the roof and saw him from a distance. Loudspeakers were blaring so that you could hear him, and the crowd was shouting, "*Viva il Duce, Viva il Duce...*"

In March 1938, after the *Anschluss*, refugees started pouring into Genoa, mostly from Austria. They told us horror stories and we were glad that we had escaped in time. Alas, in July 1938 Hitler and Mussolini met at the Brenner Pass to form the alliance that became known as the Axis, later to be joined by Japan.

For us this signaled the beginning of the end. Italy soon passed racial laws and published antisemitic propaganda. I can still see the magazine cover of *La Razza Ebraica* (The Hebrew Race). An article inside compared us to the Hottentots—whoever they were. It showed that we were different *in utero*. The cover portrayed a Roman face, then a sword, then a caricature of a Jew, then a negro. The propaganda was relentless: on posters, in newspapers, at the cinema and on the radio.

The irony was that the Italians didn't really know any Jews as there were very few in Italy, and they couldn't tell the difference between a Jew or anyone else when they met one. Papa, who had blond hair and blue eyes, had an encounter with an Italian lady on a train. She was deep in a discussion with two fellow travelers, and pointed to Papa as a good example of the typical Aryan. To avoid embarrassing her, my father waited for the two other passengers to get off before correcting her. When she still did not believe him, he pulled out his ever-present *tallis* (prayer shawl) and *tefillin* (phylacteries) to prove it.

When Jews were no longer allowed to work in Italy after July 1938, Papa and Kurt lost their jobs. My parents canceled the orders for furniture and returned what they could. We gave up the co-op and moved into a single room in Via Palestro number 15, next door to the French consulate.

Now we were refugees.

The temple and day school were shut down. Jewish children were forbidden to go to public school with their Italian counterparts. We went in the afternoon and if I was out in the afternoon with my school bag, it felt like everyone could tell I was Jewish. School was a waste of

Via Palestro in Genoa. The French Consulate is the building on the left. No. 15 is the next building on the right. Our room was on the second floor overlooking the garden between the buildings.

time because they didn't teach us very much. There was no homework, and I was used to working hard at my studies.

Living next door to the French consulate, we witnessed demonstrations against the French by Italian students, mostly teenagers. They usually came after school or on weekends, shouting "*Voliamo Nizza, Savoya, Djibouti.*" They were calling for the return of the Duchy of Savoy, which was awarded to Napoleon III for his support of the Italian unification. They also laid claim to a colonial empire in Africa. These demonstrations were frequent and would sometimes be broken up by hose-wielding firemen, who sprayed the demonstrators with strong jets of water.

On Saturday afternoons, schoolboys, some as young as 6 would parade through town, carrying toy guns. It made my parents sad. The children were led by the *Camicia Nere*, the black-shirted Fascists. In school, we were taught about the *Fascio* (the sheath of wheat, symbol of the Italian Black Shirts) and the fascist motto, "In unity there is strength." It fascinated me to see how totalitarian regimes packaged their ideas for children to make their fascist ideals seem good for society.

I was isolated from my friends because the dayschool was closed. There was a beautiful garden that was visible from my window, where children romped with their friends and their dog. I so much would have liked to play with them. Instead, I was trapped inside, looking out.

There was a lovely park on a steep hillside near the Via Palestro. In my tenth summer I was finally granted the freedom to go out by myself, a freedom I treasured. Kurt still had the camera he had received for his bar mitzvah, and photography now intrigued me. There was a children's photographer in the park who was always there with his camera at the ready to photograph parents and children. Once he had me sit on his lap, but when I felt his hands on my thighs I knew something was not right. I climbed off immediately and never went back to his area of the park.

Another time, a middle-aged man started following me. I was fleet of foot, ran, dodged and lost him. After that I became more careful, but I did not tell Mama about these incidents since I feared that she would not let me go out alone again.

In October 1938, the infamous Munich agreement was signed between France and England on one side and Germany and Italy on the other, ceding the Sudetenland to Germany. Despite British Prime Minister Chamberlain's assurances that this treaty guaranteed "peace in our time" for Europe, the talk in my house was that war was inevitable. We had felt for a long time that Hitler would not stop. As young as I was, I understood and fully expected war.

It was only a matter of time.

During that year the Italians kept calling my parents to the Questura, sort of a combination police station and city hall. The officials made it clear they wanted us to leave. The United States would not have us because we weren't qualified. First you had to have an affidavit; then you had to wait your turn on the quota system based on your country of origin. I found out later that America essentially closed its doors to Jews.

I remember poring over maps with my family, looking up every little country in Central and South America. That was one way to learn geography. Papa would run from one consulate to another. Nobody wanted us. We were trapped. We didn't know about the Evian Conference, where the nations of the civilized world closed their doors to all Jewish refugees and ignored our plight.

The only place that would accept Jews was Shanghai. Many times I went down to the harbor to see people off. Since Genoa is a major port, there were always ships sailing for different parts of the world. The lucky ones got to leave for the U.S., Canada, Argentina, Australia, South Africa or even Portugal. My family did not have the means to sail for Shanghai and there was no outside help.

In desperation, and after months of fruitless attempts to find safe haven, my parents decided to try to enter France illegally, without visas. Sometime in February 1939, we packed what few belongings we still had and left for Ventimiglia, the border town on the Italian side—to wait for an opportunity to cross into France.

NICE
We Are Refugees

We stayed in a hotel in Ventimiglia for almost two months and ate lots of risotto, the cheapest and most filling item on the restaurant menu. Finally, on a Saturday morning in April 1939, the Italian station master, who'd been cultivated by my father, told us that the next day, Sunday, there would be no passport control at the French border because his counterpart had the day off.

Immediately, my parents shipped our meager belongings to Nice and prepared us for the crossing. Mama thought I would look more casual if I wore an apron, a dirndl, and made me put one on. She didn't realize that this style would mark us as Viennese and that we were in a Mediterranean country where only cooks and housewives wore aprons. I stuck out like a sore thumb.

On Sunday, a beautiful spring day, we walked to the railroad station to catch the train to Menton, the closest French border town. We had no luggage–Papa had a little briefcase and Mama took a large purse. That was all. The ride took about 30 minutes and, as promised, no one checked our papers.

In Menton, we took a bus to Nice, the largest and closest city in the area. Papa, Mama, Kurt and I sat in the back of an empty bus. Papa asked the conductor for four tickets to Nice in his broken French. The conductor hesitated and looked us over, one at a time. I was scared for even I could see he knew we were illegals. Our lives were in his hands. Would he hand us over to the police or would he be compassionate and let us in? After what seemed like a long time, he handed us the tickets without saying a word. I heaved a sigh of relief. For the moment, we were safe.

Taken from the park overlooking the Nice harbor with the Promenade des Anglais on the left.

My new birth certificate with the name Sara added as a middle name as required by the Germans.

Once in Nice, our first stop was the Comité d'Assistance aux Réfugiés (CAR), subsidized by funds from the American Jewish Joint Distribution Committee (the JDC–usually called the Joint). It was at 2, Boulevard Victor Hugo, a good walk from the bus station, but when we got there the office was closed because it was Sunday.

By the time we made this discovery, it was time for lunch. Mama, who'd packed oranges for the trip, brought them out, and we ate them in the office building hallway as we sat on the steps. We didn't want people to notice a family of four eating "on the lam," and disposing the skins in the public trash bins, so we left the skins on a radiator in the office building.

When we were done, we walked across town to the subsidized restaurant for refugees. We didn't know it was closed on Sunday evenings, and so we stood in the middle of the street, wondering what to do next.

We could not go to a regular hotel because, under French law, the management would have to ask for our papers and inform the police of our arrival. As luck would have it, someone spotted us and, in Yiddish, asked whether we needed a place to stay. He took us to a hotel that charged extra for not informing the police, and the next day we went back to the CAR office. Since the *Anschluss* we were officially considered ex-Austrians because Austria had ceased to exist as an independent country. Once we filled out all the required forms, CAR assigned someone to accompany us to the police station to request political asylum that was immediately granted.

The first order of the day was to find affordable housing, for our limited resources were rapidly running out. My parents found a room in the old section of town, near the harbor, five minutes walking distance from the Mediterranean. The room was in an apartment shared by three or four other families, all of whom had kitchen privileges. What I remember most about that place were the cockroaches. They were big and black and when you walked around at night, both inside and outside the house, you could hear them crunch underfoot. When you went into the kitchen at night and turned on the light, the floor was black and completely covered with them. So when we had to go into the kitchen, we would go in, turn on the light and wait fifteen minutes. By then the roaches had crawled back into their hiding places and the coast was clear.

Since Mama had a holy terror of vermin she did her very best to keep our room free of them. She scrubbed and cleaned everything and then put a rag soaked in naphthalene or some other chemical under the door. Whenever we closed the door we had to push the rag against the crack at the bottom so the critters could not come back in.

Mama would go into a tizzy whenever she saw Kurt talk to one of the tenants, a prostitute. Although this woman did not bring her customers to the apartment, Mama did not like him to talk to her. He had just turned 16 and Mama had long conversations with him in code language so that I, at the ripe old age of 10, would not understand what they were talking about. I figured out what was going on, but frankly, I had little interest in the subject. Mama would refer to a prostitute as a "7-3-6," and, interestingly, I don't remember Papa ever discussing these issues with Kurt.

My parents were tough on Kurt, who had a strict curfew at 10 P.M. Once, when he came home at 11, my parents locked him out. He stood outside the building talking to my parents through the window. They let him in eventually, but not before giving him a very hard time.

In spring and summer of 1939, Nice was filled with refugees of all stripes: Jews and anti-Nazi non-Jews, some wealthy, some not. One of them, an Austrian aristocrat, Count Starhemberg, frequently associated with Jews. There was also a group of former secondary school professors from Germany, all Jewish, who let it be known through the CAR that they were willing to give free courses in French and English. Since some of the refugees were preparing to immigrate to English-speaking countries, it made sense. I jumped at the opportunity to learn French. Both Kurt and I signed up.

Classes were offered three mornings a week. We would take the long walk to the teachers' hotel across town, in the newer section of the city. Initially classes were filled, but gradually people dropped out until Kurt and I were the only ones left. French grammar did not faze me, as I had already mastered Italian. I was very motivated and studied my grammar, did my homework and attended classes faithfully. At bedtime I practiced by telling myself stories in French, though my vocabulary was limited.

To complement my grammar classes, Papa enrolled me at the local elementary school. He went to the principal, told her that I did not know a word of French and that I was taking private classes. He asked if I could attend school in the afternoons to hear French spoken, with the proviso that I not be responsible for homework. The principal agreed.

In school, I listened attentively to what was being said. One classmate was bilingual because she had Italian parents and she became my interpreter. Within two months, I was able to follow what was going on. The first poem I was able to understand was *"Les Pauvres Gens"* by Victor Hugo. When I told my interpreter the gist of the poem, she enthusiastically raised her hand and the whole class triumphed with me. After that things got easier.

The girls in my class were very nice. One came up to me, pointed to me and said *"toi"* (you), and then pointed to herself and said *"moi"* (me), and then linked her hands together as she said *"amis"* (friends). My classmates called me *l'Autrichienne* (the Austrian girl).

When school officially began, I was able to get into a regular French class for my age and to keep up with the other students. During all that time we continued to speak German at home. The only casualty was my Italian. With no reinforcement, I lost most of it. (I often think this method is a good model for teaching English to immigrant children in America: total immersion plus private tutoring in grammar for six months or a year, regardless of the language spoken at home.)

When school was out, I went to the beach every afternoon for three glorious months. I had turned 11 and Mama let me go out by myself. The beach in Nice was not like the sandy beaches of the Caribbean. It was full of big stones, no sand in sight. The rocks were hard to walk on and painful, too, because they were very hot.

The Promenade des Anglais in the newer part of town was an elegant avenue that ran along the shore, almost to the harbor. Along its route were privately run beaches that had jute-covered wooden boardwalks leading down to the water. These paid beaches were lined with beach chairs and little cafés and out of my financial reach. I swam on the other side of the harbor near the *vieille ville*, the old part of town. There the beach was free, if less glamorous.

Since I did not like to roast in the hot Mediterranean sun, I spent hours in the water. Although Mama had given me swimming lessons in Vienna, I did not have the confidence to actually swim, so I practiced all the right movements for the breaststroke as I held on to a pier. One day, an old gentleman, who was watching me, told me that I clearly knew how to swim. He waded over and held up my chin and let me swim to prove it to myself. He was right. I could swim, and after that, I would swim parallel to the shore since I was alone and there were no lifeguards.

I loved to float on my back, rocked by the gentle waves and looking up at the sky. There was nothing in the world but the sea, the blue sky,

The Promenade des Anglais on the Bay of the Angels.

sometimes a wisp of a cloud, and me. It was a wonderful feeling of peace and beauty that I attempt to recreate every chance I get.

As people fled Germany, Austria and Italy, stories of daring escapes over the mountains or around the shores of the Italian and French Riviera began to circulate. I imagined that if I had to escape by sea I would have to swim under water, so I trained myself to hold my breath for as long as possible. I also trained myself to swim for endurance rather than speed. When I hold my breath under water today I remember why I taught myself to do that.

Finding a bathing suit for me was a problem because we could not afford to buy one. During that first summer, while I was still flat-chested, I could get away with swimming in my panties. The following year, Mama draped a scarf over my chest like a halter top.

We soon moved away from the harbor area to get away from the roaches and the prostitute. We rented a room near the Place Garibaldi, also in the older part of town. That apartment was also filled with refugee families, one per room, with shared kitchen privileges, but I don't remember eating any cooked meals there. Except for a light breakfast, we mostly ate at the subsidized restaurant.

During May, every square in Nice was decorated with colored lanterns. The cafés put their tables out on the sidewalks and public squares as music blared from loudspeakers. *España,* a composition by Emmanuel Chabrier was frequently broadcast across the Place Garibaldi, and every time I hear it now I think of those days. Sometimes there was dance music and people would dance. For the price of a glass of lemonade you could sit at a table for hours, absorbing the fragrance of spring and savoring the soft night air.

That was *la douce France.* The spring and summer of 1939 were the last seasons of peace before all hell broke loose.

Unfortunately my parents ventured out in the evening only on rare occasions. They never took walks along the Promenade des Anglais where everyone would congregate in the evenings, to stroll, chat with friends or just sit and listen to the waves. For some reason my parents felt that we all had to be in after dark, even in those cramped quarters–though fresh air, music and companionship were simple, free pleasures. One of the benefits of socializing with the other refugees would have been access to valuable information. What my parents didn't realize was that anything they could find out could be useful to our survival.

That summer, Kurt was hired by the CAR as a doorman and errand boy. The job came with an old bicycle, and boy did he love it! He would

Place Garibaldi in Nice.
We had a room nearby on the rue Cassini.

Papa in Nice, Place Garibaldi, spring 1939.

Kurt, Place Garibaldi, same day.
(This is the photo we enlarged into a portrait.)

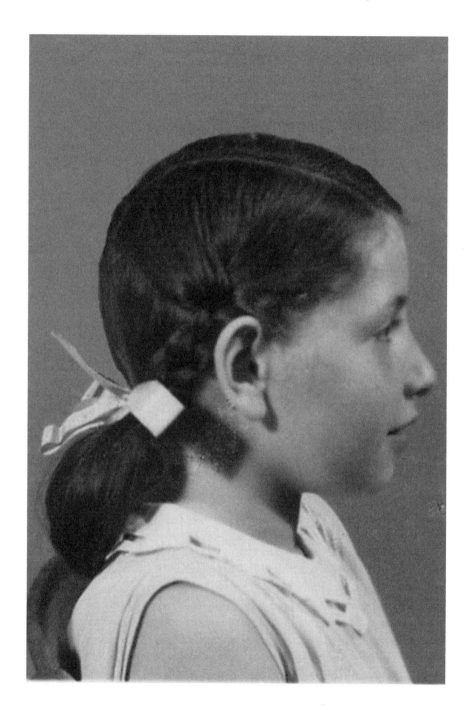

My identity photo in Nice.
It had to be in profile to expose the ear.

whistle to the tune of "Shalom Aleichem" to get Mama's attention—we now lived on the second floor—because he wanted her to look out the window to watch him riding his bike, hands free.

Kurt was a pleasant and conscientious employee and well liked by everyone. He would occasionally go to the beach off the Promenade des Anglais and hang out with people his age. One young girl in the group, Edith Steinmetz whose nickname was Putzi, was always surrounded by boys. She was 18, wore lipstick, and her body gleamed with suntan oil. She had a nice tan and never went into the water. She just sat on the beach and flirted with all the boys. As a flat-chested kid with pigtails, I stayed away and went swimming by myself.

There were lots of kids in Nice. The CAR wanted to do something nice for us and so treated us to a screening of *Snow White*, the popular Disney film that was released while we were still in Italy and one I really wanted to see. It was, indeed, a special treat.

Poverty was our constant companion. I often asked Papa for an ice cream cone during those hot summer days. It cost 10 centimes. Papa would say that he would have to buy one for each of us, that came to 40 centimes and we could not afford that. It never occurred to him that we could all share a scoop of the delicious treat!

As a result ice cream was reserved for special occasions. Many years later my mother invited my two little girls, then seven and nine, to an ice cream parlor in Boston. I knew what it meant to her, even if my children did not: ice cream to them was nothing special.

Other than the items in my wardrobe that Mama knitted for me, I wore hand-me-downs, including shoes from charitable organizations that gave me blisters. On the rare occasions when I found something nice to wear, Kurt took pictures of me in my new outfits, and I still have those photos!

The CAR gave a modest cash subsidy of 50 French francs to eligible families. We would joke that it was too much to die on, but not enough to live on. Even with the subsidized restaurant and Kurt's modest job, life was difficult because we were not allowed to work. Mining and agriculture were the only two industries open to foreigners. Since Mama could sew and Papa knew some tailoring, my parents took in mending and altered clothing for the wealthier refugees. They turned cuffs, sewed on buttons and resized garments.

Eventually my parents found an apartment in a suburban area, half an hour walking distance from the last streetcar stop on the Boulevard de l'Observatoire. Aside from the healthier air and greater privacy, my parents had been anxious to get out of the shared apartment because

Refugee children in front of the subsidized restaurant. (I'm in the front, left.)

they did not like the company Kurt was keeping. They felt that one young man in particular was a bad influence on him. At least, that's what they said.

The new apartment, at number 63, Boulevard de l'Observatoire, had two rooms, a kitchen and a toilet. It also had a large terrace and a view of the section of St. Roch down below. The building was built into the mountain and had two floors above street level and two floors below. We had the second floor below street level. Our "spare" room had mildew and was unusable so all four of us slept in the larger room. Mama and I shared a single box spring—my head was at her feet. Papa and Kurt slept on the stone floor on featherbeds and blankets. The kitchen served as the living/dining/kitchen/laundry/homework room.

The worst thing about that apartment was that you had to walk up a very steep hill to get to it, as it was literally built into the mountain. On hot summer days the hike was murder. In the summer of 1940 when I went down to the sea for my daily swim, the one-hour walk from the beach negated the refreshing experience. Many times I gave up swimming because it was too hot to make the trip back up the mountain.

In addition to doing alterations, my parents began taking in laundry. They picked up the dirty laundry at the hotels, carried it home, washed it and dried it on our nice terrace. Mama did the ironing and mending and my parents then carried the clothing back to the hotels. To hide their economic activity, Mama covered the laundry with fresh vegetables. Initially Papa helped with tailoring, pick up and delivery, but after he was arrested and taken to Les Milles, a French concentration camp, Mama continued on her own. I often helped her out and carried the bundles to and from the hotels when I was not in school.

While we still lived near the Place Garibaldi, my parents signed me up at the Ecole Papon, *Cours Moyen Première Année*—essentially the fourth grade. My teacher was Mme. Provençal, a fiercely patriotic woman who taught us songs from the French Revolution and the Napoleonic era. She constantly ranted how the French had been making butter while the Germans were building guns.

It was the winter of the *drôle de guerre,* or phony war, with occasional skirmishes along the Maginot Line, with its stationary guns facing Germany. But there not much action until May 1940, when the Germans attacked France with a blitzkrieg, the lightning war. We were taught to put on gas masks, because the Germans used mustard gas in World War I, *La Grande Guerre* (the Great War). No one expected a second world war to follow so soon on the heels of the first.

Academically I held my own. I was proud because other refugee children my age were placed in lower grades because their French was weak, and I was placed with my peers. We were given monthly tests in every subject. Scores were added up and students were ranked on the basis of their total score. The one with the highest score was first, the next one second, and so forth. Seating in class was based on this ranking, so that the good students sat in front and the weak ones sat in the back.

During the first grading period I was ranked 19th out of a class of 44 students. The following month I moved up to 16th, then 12th, then seventh, seventh again, then fifth. During the last month of school I finally ranked first, which did not please Mme. Provençal. Instead of the usual words of encouragement and praise, she told me that the only reason I was first was that the student who normally achieved that rank was gone. It was unkind to say, and it hurt. This teacher also withheld information about entrance exams for the *lycée*, the French academic secondary system. At the time, 12 was the cut-off age for taking the exam and I turned 12 at the end of that academic year. It was now evident that she had less than my best interests at heart.

The girl who usually placed first happened to be my good friend. Simone Bertolo was blonde, petite, small featured and always neatly dressed. I sometimes visited her on the rue de la République, where she lived with her parents. I don't know whether her place deserved the designation "apartment." They had two immaculate but tiny rooms, and Simone slept across the hall in a space not much bigger than a closet. She was an only child and her parents told me that they were atheists. While they called me *la petite juive*, the little Jewish girl, they were clearly not antisemitic and were always very nice to me. In June 1940, her family fled Nice, fearing the German invasion during the collapse of France.

I kept in touch with Simone over the years. In 1970-71, my family lived in Nice for a year during an academic sabbatical, and she invited us all to dinner in her new apartment near the Ecole Bischoffsheim. She never earned her *Baccalauréat*, was married to a truck driver, had one son, and did the bookkeeping for her husband. She was as sweet as when she was a child and seemed happy. Her mother, then a widow, still lived in the hovel on the rue de la République.

After we moved to the Boulevard de l'Observatoire, I was allowed to finish the term at the Ecole Papon. The following year I registered at the Ecole Bischoffsheim, a good 30-minute walk at the bottom of the hill, near the last tramway stop.

Cours Moyen Première Année. I'm fifth from left in the back row. Simone Bertolo is third from left, front row.

The principal told me to take the *Cours Moyen Deuxième Année*—the next grade level, and warned me that if I couldn't keep up with the others, I would be put back to the *Cours Moyen Première Année*. On the first day of class, the new teacher called out various math problems—addition, subtraction, multiplication, division and fractions. We wrote the answers on our little slate boards and held them up for her to see. At the end of the morning session, the teacher called me over and told me that I knew more than the other students in her class and that I should go to the *Cours Supérieur Première Année*—sixth grade. That was the class that prepared students for the *Certificat d'Etudes* and also for the entrance exam to the *lycée*. The course was taught by the principal, a petite woman in her late 40s or early 50s, who wore her black hair pulled back into a bun.

Academically, that year was a complete waste. Once you know how to count, read, write and spell, how many times can you learn it again? On top of that, I was frequently absent because Mama needed an interpreter whenever she had to go to the Préfecture, so I missed monthly tests. I always ended up sitting in the rear of the classroom as *non-classée* and in the company of girls more interested in boys than they were in getting an education.

The age spread in the class went from 11 to 15, with the younger students preparing for the entrance exam to the *lycée* and the older ones repeating the class, several times if necessary, until they could pass the tests for the *Certificat d'Etudes*—the minimum requirement if you wanted to get a job. The official school photograph shows the age spread. The teacher had her *chou-chous* (favorites) and made no bones about it.

I was bored. There was a library at the rear of the classroom with books by La Comtesse de Ségur and Hector Malot. The former talked about the lives of aristocrats—where the disaster of the day was a dog dirtying a little girl's new white dress. Our teacher often read to us from the novel *Mon Oncle et Mon Curé* (*My Uncle and My Priest*). It was the story of a sassy young girl coming of age who was caught in a battle between her uncle and her priest. The priest wouldn't let her read certain books in her uncle's library.

My world was falling apart and I was supposed to be interested in such insipid stuff? The teacher took no interest in me; it was as if I did not exist. I had a few friends in school, but we didn't socialize outside. They were nice girls and good kids, who were not obsessed with boys, but still they were definitely not *lycée* material. In the end, I passed the *Certificat d'Etudes* and took an optional swimming test to

Cours Supérieur Première Année. Spring 1941. (I am 12 years old, in the front on the left.)

earn a *brevet sportif.* I was proud of that honor, though I didn't think that doing a few laps in a pool was a difficult test.

At one point, I managed to get hold of *Monsoon,* a novel by Louis Bromfield that was made into a movie called *When the Rains Came,* starring Lana Turner and Richard Burton. The story was set in India under the British and showed the interaction of the different layers of society in India, from the Brahmins to the Untouchables and the ruling British colonials.

Everyone in the book was very class-conscious, but when the rains came, the only thing that mattered was courage, ability and above all, character—in a pinch, class meant nothing. When the monsoon hit, the whole elaborate social structure collapsed. The book made me aware of social class and I asked Mama which "class" we belonged to. Her response was *"gut buergerlich,"* the solid middle-class bourgeoisie. Her father had been a highly respected and wealthy businessman before the Great War, and she identified with that. After the war, when I hit rock bottom, I decided to do everything in my power to get back to where my family belonged.

Soon after, the French declared war on Germany on September 3, 1939, Papa was arrested as an enemy alien. He was sent to the Camp Les Milles, near Marseille. Ironically, he was interned with Nazi Germans because the French made no distinction between those fleeing Nazism and Nazis. All were foreigners; all were thrown in together.

Papa was arrested a few weeks after my 11th birthday. After that I had almost no contact with him, since Mama did all the letter writing. While Papa's letters sent me kisses along with injunctions to listen to Mama and be good, the letters were addressed solely to Mama.

In June 1940, when France fell in what they call *La Débacle,* everything turned to chaos. Throughout that winter there were constant blackouts. Blue light bulbs were required, and all windows were covered with blue opaque paper so that bomber pilots would not see the city from the sky.

Rumors were rife. Somewhere, Mama picked up information that Jews were to be taken into protective custody by the French and thought we were supposed to show up at police headquarters. At the same time, the government of the Third Republic fled Paris for Bordeaux—the French could not even protect their own. A flood of refugees streamed down from Alsace-Lorraine and other combat zones in the north.

What did Mama do? She went to downtown Nice accompanied by 15-year-old Rosette, our neighbor, to find out where we were supposed to go. She had already packed our bags and was ready to go wherever they sent us.

Mama left with Rosette around 2 P.M. At dinnertime, Rosette returned, alone, and told me they were unsuccessful in their attempt to get help from the authorities. She described how, by late afternoon, Mama stood in the middle of the road in front of a truck, waving her arms trying to stop the driver to hitch a ride. The story did not make any sense, nor did Rosette. In the end Rosette decided to leave Mama and go home. She had no idea where Mama had gone.

I waited in our empty apartment where there was nothing to eat. At 10 P.M., when Mama was still not home, I went looking for her. I started down the Boulevard de l'Observatoire, but it was pitch black and I could not see a thing. Until that night I had always been afraid of the dark. Groping my way down the boulevard with real things to worry about, my fear left me. After walking a short distance, I realized that I could not accomplish anything, so I returned to the apartment. An hour later, I went to a Jewish neighbor's house. They were very gracious, gave me some food and invited me to spend the night.

By midnight, just as I was about to settle down to sleep, Mama arrived. She was furious with me, and bawled me out for going to the neighbors, eating dinner and going to bed. How dare I do such things when she was out there wandering in the streets? I quickly dressed and left with her. I have no idea where Kurt was that night, but he must have been safe because Mama did not express any concern about him.

It was a good thing the protective custody Mama sought did not materialize or I would not be here. France fell more quickly than anyone had anticipated. As soon as the armistice was signed, the victors did not waste any time. The Vichy puppet regime was established in the southern half of France, often referred to as Free France, while the northern half of France and the entire Atlantic coastline were under direct German military command.

Soon after the fall of France, Papa was released along with all the other enemy aliens. We were overjoyed to see him, but he had some kind of infection on his belly and had to be hospitalized. He was sent to the hospital in Purpans, quite a distance from Nice. There they kept the wound open with a shunt in order to drain the infection. He was there for a month and we went to visit him almost daily until he was released. Had he stayed in the hospital longer, it might have saved his life.

It was July 1940, and I had just turned 12. Papa was home for only a few days when there came a knock on the door at 6 A.M. while everyone was still asleep. The order from Vichy was to arrest all Jewish men above the age of 17. Kurt had just turned 17. Now two French policemen were at the door to arrest Papa and Kurt. The police gave them 30 minutes to get dressed, pack their bags and say goodbye to Mama and me.

That was the last time I saw Papa.

When Papa was arrested he took along the silver pocket watch that so enchanted me as a child. At my request Papa would push the knob, and the watch would play a lovely chime. It was attached to a gold chain that he left behind. I now know that when people arrived in Auschwitz or other collection points or labor camps, they were ordered to give their valuables to the guards for "safekeeping." I cannot help but wonder whether some old German, playing the chime for his grandchild, boasts about how it came into his possession. Does he say "This one, sonny, I took from an old Jew just before I shoved him into the gas chamber." Does the new owner ever feel remorse or shame? Whenever I pass in front of a fine jewelry store, I still look for that watch. (The last time I saw a similar pocket watch, the asking price was $5,000.)

Kurt and Papa were sent to Gurs, a notorious concentration camp near Pau in the Pyrénées. There, in order to earn some cash, they did laundry for those camp inmates who had a bit of money. Washing clothes in that setting must have been hard work, especially during the winter months.

In Mama's papers I came across a postcard sent from Gurs by my Uncle Rudolf (the same uncle who threw her out when she and Papa were engaged). He wrote that he ran into Kurt in the camp, and described how painfully thin he looked. I still have trouble reading that postcard because my eyes always fill with tears.

Meanwhile the noose tightened around Mama and me. She was frequently called to the Préfecture, where our residence permit was renewed for increasingly shorter periods of time. Every three months became every two weeks. Since Mama did not speak French, I always had to go with her as the interpreter. As a result, during the school year I missed a lot of class time.

These meetings with the French authorities were a farce. Because we were not allowed to work, we had to show that we had enough resources to live on. The standard procedure was to go to the CAR, borrow 5,000 French francs and then show that money to the authorities. The next

In front of 2, Boulevard Victor Hugo. I'm 12 years old.

day you returned the money to the CAR, who gave the francs to another refugee for the same reason. It was a Kafkaesque world—those same 5000 francs saved hundreds of refugees.

Mama worked hard to keep body and soul together as she continued to take in laundry. That winter I spent my Christmas vacation ironing shirts for her and helping her carry the bundles to and from the hotels. When I went back to school in January, we were assigned a composition about what we did during our vacation. I concocted a story about visiting my grandmother in the countryside so it would read like the compositions the other girls were writing. I was too ashamed to tell the truth.

Food rationing became more severe after the German Occupation. Our ration cards were stamped with the *J* for *Juif,* as were the rest of our documents. That was also when the names Sara for women and Abraham for men were added to Jewish identity cards. As a teenager I was entitled to more food than the adults and got one-and-a half pounds of marmalade or jam while Mama got half a pound. This added up to a full can of jam that we sent to Papa in camp while we did without. We did the same thing with sardines or tuna and other items that could easily be shipped. Typically the French guards in the camp helped themselves to at least a portion of the package while Papa and Kurt got what was left. To compensate for the lack of food, I had to swallow cod liver oil and calcium granules.

Between my inadequate diet and because maintaining proper dental hygiene was impossible, I began to lose my teeth. Whenever I had a toothache, my tooth was pulled without anesthesia—the practice at the time. When children in the dental clinic rinsed their mouths, they were given an unwashed cup used by other children. After their surgeries, the children would stand before a sink in a large hall with blood dripping from their faces. It was an awful sight.

In the spring of 1941, when Papa and Kurt had been in Gurs for a year, we received a postcard with the usual news, but at the edge of the card Kurt had scribbled, "Mordechai is coming." Mordechai was Kurt's Hebrew name, and we wondered what it meant. We did not have to wait long to find out. A couple of weeks later Kurt showed up at the door. He had escaped from Gurs and told us Papa would soon follow. At the time I believed that. Now I realize that, without Kurt, there was no chance Papa could have escaped. After our initial joy at having Kurt back, we realized it was unsafe for him to stay with us because the police would come looking for him.

After many inquiries and much searching we found a farm outside Nice where a number of young Zionists were on *Hachshara,* working the land and preparing to move to Mandate Palestine, the *Yishuv*. Kurt spent about six weeks there and recovered a bit from camp life. A few surviving photos show him in the company of young people looking happy and well fed.

However, all the people at the farm were "legal." And since Kurt's status as an escapee jeopardized all the others, he was asked to leave. Putzi Steinmetz's father was something of a wheeler-dealer and strongly recommended that Kurt join the *Prestataires*—foreign volunteers who served France as non-combatants under French military command. Kurt was issued a uniform, but kept his ID card with the dangerous *J* stamped on it.

Eventually he was shipped off with other Jewish men to work in a quarry in the southwestern part of France. We thought this was an improvement over Gurs. Mr. Steinmetz assured us that Kurt would be safe there. Of course this turned out to be a major mistake that ended up costing Kurt his life. He should have gone underground with false papers, to join the resistance.

While Kurt was still in Nice, I once went to town with him. He wore a white shirt and gray slacks and I wore a white blouse and gray skirt. I thought we looked special in our matching outfits. He was six feet tall and, I thought, good-looking. I had just turned 13 and didn't realize I was becoming a teenager. We were beginning to appreciate each other and began to take pleasure in each other's company. I had been too young until then to appreciate him. He told Mama that girls my age are usually not good looking, but thought I looked nice. I was very proud to be seen with him, and he was always very protective of "his little sister."

When school started in September 1941, I was promoted to the *Cours Supérieur Deuxième Année*, seventh grade. At that time the French school system had two parallel tracks: the primary and the secondary. If you missed out on the entrance exam to the *lycée* you could continue in the primary system for three more years after the *Certificat d'Etudes*. The curriculum was similar to that of the *lycée*, but took longer and was watered down. Except for our English course we had the same teacher for all our subjects, while the *lycée* assigned different professors for each subject. Even so, at last, there was more educational substance there, and I was learning new things.

My teacher was Mme. Brun, an angel in black. She was in mourning for her only child, who had died of meningitis. She was an exceptional woman and I kept in touch with her for many years.

Kurt, 18, in Nice, right after his escape from the camp of Gurs.
He is very thin.

Kurt, two months after his escape, with friends at Hachshara.
He is in the middle with tie.

With Mama on the terrace.

Me with the neighbor's cat on our terrace. I am 13 years old.
My father's only comment from the French concentration camp
upon receiving my picture: "The dress is too short."

She was kind and took an interest in me. I remember one day, when Kurt showed up at school wearing his French uniform, that she spoke to him with kindness.

Mme. Brun started us on English, and I imitated her pronunciation until a real English teacher was hired. The new teacher's accent was quite different and I realized that Mme. Brun had incorrect pronunciation, so I quickly changed mine.

In the meantime, my frequent trips to the Préfecture only further caused my school work to suffer. But not for long. The Department of the Maritime Alps and Nice were soon closed to Jews, and so we were forced to leave. Had we stayed, the Germans would have deported us to the death camps once the Italian troops left.

America entered the war in 1942 after the December 1941 attack on Pearl Harbor. We heard that President Roosevelt declared that by 1944 America would have many ships, tanks and bombers. I didn't think we would last that long, that it would be too late for the Jews. Unfortunately I was right. The mass deportations had already begun.

The struggle for survival, for food, for money, the worry about Papa and Kurt, the depressing letters from camp—that were heavily censored with black indelible ink–the drudgery of hauling other people's laundry up and down the hill, did not make for happy times. An 18-year old girl in my neighborhood once told me that, compared to her, I had no worries—maybe she was pregnant and unwed—what could I say to her? I was keenly aware of our precarious situation.

In April 1942, we left Nice to hide in Montlaur, a little village in the southwestern part of France.

MONTLAUR
The Farm Hand

In the winter-spring of 1942, Kurt was working in a quarry with other *Prestataires,* all Jewish refugees. The quarry was located in a semi-arid region of southwestern France near Carcassonne, a town known for its well-preserved fortified medieval city. Knowing that we needed to get out of Nice, Kurt contacted the mayor of a nearby village, Montlaur, and asked for a residence permit for Mama and me. Amazingly, he got it.

We took a train from Nice to Carcassonne and a bus from there to Montlaur. When the daily bus arrived in the village, it was always an event. There were at least two dozen children swarming around the bus together with villagers who came to pick up packages or meet relatives. Kurt came to greet us.

Montlaur was a village of approximately 900 people where everyone knew everyone else, and minded each others' business. Needless to say, as strangers we attracted attention. Nothing was hidden, and nothing could be hidden.

The village was off a cul-de-sac on the road connecting Carcassonne to Lagrasse. The village's only cash crop was grapes used for making ordinary table wine. There were a few choice vineyards in the region, where sweet muscatel grapes were grown and they received more attention and care. During the war, an effort was made to grow wheat and corn on distant fields normally left fallow, about an hour's travel time by oxcart.

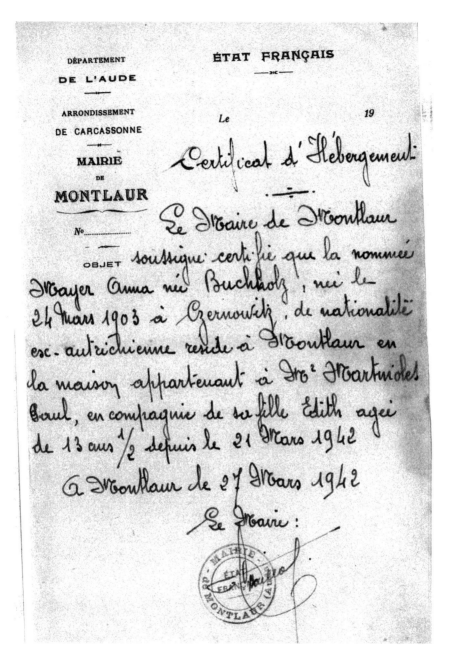

DÉPARTEMENT

DE L'AUDE

ARRONDISSEMENT

DE CARCASSONNE

MAIRIE

DE

MONTLAUR

ÉTAT FRANÇAIS

Le   19

Certificat d'Hébergement

Le Maire de Montlaur soussigné certifie que la nommée Mayer Anna née Buchholz, née le 24 Mars 1903 à Czernowitz, de nationalité ex-autrichienne reside à Montlaur en la maison appartenant à Mr Martinoles Saul, en compagnie de sa fille Edith agée de 13 ans 1/2 depuis le 21 Mars 1942

A Montlaur de 27 Mars 1942

Le Maire :

Our Montlaur residence permit from the town's mayor.

As you drove into the village from Carcassonne, you came upon the main square. To the right was a high wall with broken glass on top. It bordered the vineyards and park of the *Château*. This is how the villagers referred to the large manor house owned by the Niermans family. Rumor had it that Mr. Niermans won the estate at a gambling table, but who knew? It was an interesting rumor. To the left was a large, classically designed building with the city hall in the middle, the boys' eight-year elementary school on the left and the girls' school on the right. There were benches where one usually found old men sitting in the shade. Several streets led away from the square.

The village had two cafés: *le grand café* and *le petit café*. The smaller attracted older men playing *la belote*, a card game I never learned. The larger café had a dance hall that was open on Saturday nights. When I first came to the village I went with the local girls and learned the dance steps by watching people on the dance floor. As the war progressed, locals decided dancing was inappropriate.

Kurt was able to rent an old stone house from the Martinoles, well-to-do peasants. It was on the Grand'rue, an unpaved street that turned to mud when it rained. The house had no running water, no toilet, no gas, and no stove. There was a large room at ground level that had a worn tile floor and a large open hearth where I cooked our meals. There was a room upstairs that Mama and I shared, and the loft above that was used by Kurt once he joined us. We used bags of jute filled with straw called *paillasses* as our mattresses. On average, the straw was replaced about once a year, when the old stuffing turned to dust.

Cooking was an adventure. I would put a cookpot on a tripod placed over burning wood. This was complicated because I did not know how to build a fire, and I had nothing with which to start one. Because the wood at my disposal was green and not dry, it took me hours to get the fire going—and every fire I built filled the kitchen with smoke. I blamed myself for my failures until I realized I lacked the basic tools—paper, dry grasses, dry twigs or other kindling, and, of course, dry wood.

There was a *remise*, a space adjacent to this large room, that had a dirt floor and was uninhabitable. The villagers used theirs as stables or for storage. We used it to store the wood for cooking and for our human waste bucket.

Getting rid of human waste was a problem for everyone in the village. Because of the lack of real sewers and sumps, the local brook was used as a dump. There were special toilet buckets with rims and lids available, but we couldn't afford to buy one and used an old pail.

View of Montlaur from the hill behind the village.

The street where I lived.

Every morning the village housewives carried their buckets down to the stream. I was too embarrassed to carry our open bucket, so I would wait until the bucket was full (and quite heavy) and go down at night to avoid being seen. In summertime the stream was reduced to a trickle, so that everyone's waste ended up on its banks and it sat there until the rains came in the fall and washed it away. The area stank to high heaven.

The worst thing about our house was the infestation of mice and rats. Every night they came out and nibbled at our bread, leaving their droppings nearby. We had so little food that I simply cut off the part they had touched so I could eat the rest. In fact, rats were a problem throughout the village. People would put out rat traps. I once saw one filled with five or six rats. The villagers poured gasoline on the rats and set them on fire. There must be more humane ways to get rid of rodents, but the villagers did what they could. Poison was not used.

Water was scarce, especially during the summer. Water for washing and cooking came from the fountain in the square half a block from the cottage. For drinking water we walked for 10 or 15 minutes to a pipe that came from a spring. Before mealtimes, there was always a line of villagers. The water came out of the pipe in a thin stream. In the summer—the dry season—the fountain was open for only two hours at a time: in the morning, at noon and in the evening.

There was a town crier who provided the local news. He was handsome, about 30 years old, but had only one arm. He worked in the mayor's office and made the rounds of the town squares and water fountains, hitting his drum to alert us to his announcements. He would shout out things like, "There will be no water from 2 P.M. to 6 P.M."

Soon after we arrived in the village, Kurt got permission to leave the quarry and live with us. He found work as a farmhand at the Niermans' *Château* because there was a shortage of manpower to tend the fields and vineyards.

During the war, corn was planted to feed livestock; most people tended their own vegetable patches. The Niermans assigned us a little plot of land outside the village where we could grow our own food. Kurt and I worked at it, but when he left and the water dried up, I had no manure and nothing grew. Besides, I didn't know what I was doing and it bothered me to go out to the field in the evenings by myself.

Getting enough food to eat was a problem. The monthly food ration usually sufficed for just 20 days. In the summer and fall we supplemented our rations with locally grown produce that I bought

Kurt in the quarry.

The *Prestataire* group. Kurt is in the back, sixth from the left.

from the beautifully tended vegetable garden owned by the Noyes family. But during the winter, produce wasn't available.

The villagers supplemented their rations and the food they grew by hunting jack rabbits, or trapping them illegally when the hunting season was over. The villagers also raised chickens, a few had a cow and everyone had a pig. The pigs were slaughtered before Christmas and would provide ham and sausage for the rest of the year. After it rained, the villagers gathered snails that were eaten with garlic butter. I ate some once and was appalled when I learned they were boiled alive.

When I first got to Montlaur, I explored the outlying fields and discovered wild fig trees growing among the vineyards. I would climb the trees and delight in eating figs while gathering some to bring home, but I had to stop after the manager of the *Château* complained that I was distracting his farm workers. Once in a while I picked wild blackberries growing along the paths between the fields, but I didn't have a container to carry them in, so I was only able to take what I could hold in a scarf or apron.

Mama and I applied for jobs at the *Château*, the largest employer in the village. Work was done by hand, as it had been since the Middle Ages. We used cutters, scythes, sickles, hoes and horse-drawn plows. There were a few tractors here and there, but because gasoline was rationed and scarce, they sat idle. A man could hire himself out with his horse and earn a good day's wages plowing fields.

Once we began working, part of our pay came in the form of two liters of wine a day per person—that's a gallon of wine a day. Since we didn't drink, most of it turned to vinegar. After we had enough vinegar to feed the multitudes, the wine went to waste.

I still remember our first day at work. Mama and I were each given seed-filled bags to tie around our waists. We were also given a one-foot long stick and a regular spoon. For the next eight hours, we planted beets, working on already tilled ground with a team of six or eight women. We dug little holes with our spoons and dropped three seeds into each one, covering each hole with dirt. We used the stick to measure the distance to the next spot, where we dug the next hole, and so on.

We remained bent over as we moved from one hole to the next. We had little time to stand up to stretch and straighten our backs. By the end of that day, neither Mama nor I could stand up straight. We managed to get to a low wall on a bridge and sat down. Luckily for us, a farmhand working for the *Chateau* came by on a horse-drawn cart and offered us a ride back to the village, half an hour away. His name was Angel Rosetti.

He seemed nice enough. He was the youngest son of an Italian immigrant family that was employed at the *Château* and lived in quarters near the barns. The father and the middle son—who was single—had salaried year-round jobs. His mother milked the cow and tended to the chickens. In exchange she got milk and eggs. The oldest son was divorced. Angel was a day laborer, *un journalier* like me, and he, too, was single. Later, he paid a lot of attention to me and initially, I was flattered. I was 14 and he was 21.

A few weeks after we were hired, Mama was asked through the manager if she wanted to work as a cook for the Niermans. The family had a chambermaid, a young village woman named Georgette, so Mama wouldn't have to clean, and she was happy to accept. Working indoors at a task she was familiar with was much easier than working in the vineyards.

Mme. Niermans, a haughty elderly widow with a polio-crippled middle-aged daughter, normally lived in Paris and came to Montlaur only in the summer. But because of the German Occupation and the food shortages, she and her daughter decided to sit out the war in the village. Occasionally, her son and his family would come to visit.

As the cook, Mama got a portion of the family leftovers for her meals. If there were no leftovers, Mme. Niermans would give her an egg. Mama often brought that egg home for me. Mme. Niermans would rummage in the garbage can seeking the egg shells, and when she didn't find them, she would yell at Mama for not eating the egg. When there were extra leftovers, she stored them in a screened cube, and since there was no refrigeration, the food would be thrown out within two days. Not once did Madame offer us any food.

During the last days of the month, when the rations were gone, my breakfast often consisted of half a glass of wine and a lump of sugar. Looking back I don't know how I managed, because the work I did was physically demanding. At lunchtime, on my way back from the fields, I would stop at the baker's shop and ask her to sell me a pound of bread without ration coupons. She never gave me a full pound, but she always sold me something, usually half a pound.

Every day I walked to the stable at the *Château* to meet up with the other farmhands and the manager, *le régisseur*. He handed out our work assignments and typically I would be sent out with a group of women led by *la mousseigne*, who only spoke the local dialect, not

Me in Montlaur, shortly after my arrival.
From school girl...

…to peasant girl and farm hand. I am 14 years old.

French. She was illiterate and I did not understand her *patois*. She seemed old to me at the time, but she could not have been much more than 40, though she was all wrinkled and usually dressed in black. She was the team leader, like a foreman, and set the work pace.

I went through the whole cycle of tending vineyards. I hoed in the spring to remove weeds, attached branches to wires to support the future grapes, pruned branches and removed extra foliage to allow the sun to ripen the grapes in May or June, then harvested the grapes in the fall. The harvest was called *les vendanges*, the once-a-year cash crop that was eagerly awaited by the peasants. Everyone pitched in, including children as young as 12 who worked with the women because time was of the essence: The grapes had to be picked at their peak.

It was August and the grapes were still sour when Kurt was told by his commanding officer that he had just a day or two to rejoin his outfit. For about three months he had been "detached" from his unit of *Prestataires*.

At our request the manager of the Niermans' estate pleaded with the CO: "He is a good worker, I need him."

"If he does not show up, we will come and get you," came the reply.

Kurt had mixed feelings about leaving. After the initial joy of our family reunion in Montlaur three months earlier, Mama resumed her periodic outbursts. She never needed much to get angry, often over really minor things. Kurt was a good son. He didn't smoke, drink or mess around with girls, and worked hard for us. I don't remember him going out to the local cafés like the other men in the village. Yet Mama constantly found fault with him. She couldn't beat him anymore, because he was bigger than she was, but oh did she scream! And she had a mean tongue. She would carry on for hours, yelling and harping away.

After one nasty episode, she brought Kurt to tears. He finally yelled back at her, "When I am dead you will cry, but now you are giving me a hard time."

Kurt packed his few belongings into his new *musette*, a canvas bag the size of a small piece of hand luggage with a shoulder strap. "You'll escape," Mama said. "Yes," came the reply.

With hindsight, I believe she may have drained him of the energy he needed to resist, though it would be cruel to blame my mother for his death. The Germans killed him with the full cooperation of the French. But deep down I feel that, had she not made his life so miserable with her endless dramas and meanness, his fighting spirit would have remained high. He might have tried harder to come back to the village or hide nearby.

Early the next morning, he left. He had been looking forward to the harvest to fill up on grapes since he was always hungry, but that was not to be. Under the guise of helping my brother, the *Château* manager sent Angel to accompany him. The two of them biked to Lagrasse and Angel brought back the empty bike.

Later that morning, Mama took the bus to Lagrasse with me in tow. We arrived at the military headquarters to find many Jews milling around an open courtyard. There, a few French soldiers armed with guns stood watch. The *Prestataires* had uniforms, but no guns.

That afternoon, Kurt's unit was sent to Agde. Given the shortage of gas, the unit of perhaps a dozen men was sent out in a flat, open cart drawn by two oxen. The road they took passed within two kilometers of Montlaur, so Mama asked for permission for us to ride along. It was granted. The men were guarded by two Spaniards, each equipped with a rifle. The two drivers sat on their bench with their guns at their sides, and the rest of us sat on the flatbed with our legs dangling over the edge.

The trip must have taken almost two hours. Mama clung to Kurt and urged him to escape. He assured her that he would. In fact, there was a lot of talk about escaping. Sadly, though, it was all negative. Two of the men had escaped once, only to be caught later. They complained about the cold, about getting sick, about how hard it was to survive.

When we reached the fork in the road, Mama and I got off and kissed Kurt goodbye. We walked back to the village as Kurt and his unit continued on their fateful journey. That was the last time I saw my brother.

In my mind's eye, I have replayed that trip on the cart hundreds of times. For a long time I accepted the sequence of events because I believed we were powerless. As I got older, however, I asked myself why I hadn't said anything encouraging to him or to the other men. I was utterly dependent on my mother and dominated by her. So there I sat, listening to all the defeatist talk. Yet that day was the best day for escaping. Two Spanish civilians, both refugees from Franco's Spain, were driving the oxcart to earn a few francs. They had their backs turned to us. The oxen moved at a snail's pace. It would have been so easy to seize those guns and send the Spaniards on their way.

I remember one of the men in my brother's group. He was 40-ish, an intellectual, soft-spoken and kind. The treasure he took along with him was a valuable stamp collection reflecting the patient accumulation of a lifetime. It reminded me of Papa's pocket watch. So why didn't I speak up? Why didn't I see that the moment to run was at hand? These thoughts continue to hurt me.

Later we received several postcards from Kurt describing how he had to surrender his uniform, how he went from Agde to Bram and, finally, the last postcard arrived, the one he sent before crossing the demarcation line into German-occupied northern France to an "unknown destination."

Mama and I still had to survive. For the harvest, the government issued extra rations to the farmhands in consideration of the hard physical labor they had to do. With Papa and Kurt sent to "destination unknown" we could no longer send food to them, so we had more food. But I was still hungry and the grape harvest was great for me because I could eat grapes to my heart's content and satisfy my hunger.

I began by eating one grape at a time. Eventually, I took whole bites out of bunches of grapes and put the rest in the basket. The grapes were unwashed and had a sulfur residue on them from being sprayed to prevent mildew. The harvest lasted about 10 or 12 days and by the end of it, my mouth was sore from the acid on the grape skin. I eventually solved the problem of my burning lips by squeezing the insides of the grapes into my mouth without their touching my lips.

After the harvest, the men clipped the vine branches, the *sarments*, close to the trunk (*souche*). The women gathered the cut branches from where they had fallen, tied them into hand-sized bundles, and then tied eight bundles together to form a *fagot*. This was used as firewood, since each bundle fit neatly under the tripods in the fireplace hearth.

The branch-gathering was done in the fall, during the rainy season. It was backbreaking work, and we stood on soggy ground with wet feet, bending over to pick up the branches. Decent shoes were unavailable because of rationing and I couldn't afford the wooden shoes the peasants wore. I had no gloves, so my hands were badly scratched. The frostbite, chilblains and scratches on my hands did not heal until spring. Sometime in November, I was able to work in the barn, preparing corn for animal fodder.

One day, the manager sent me out to cut down corn stalks with a dull sickle in the company of three men. At the time, there was little field work to be had, and perhaps the manager thought he was doing me a

Kurt's last picture before he was deported. He was 19.

Kurt with some Vietnamese workers.

favor, though it was very rare that a woman would be sent out with a man's team. I really have no idea what motivated him that day.

Angel Rosetti was one of the men on the team. After Kurt was gone, Angel became more aggressive, and was always trying to steal kisses. If someone saw us together he would say: "*piano bassano*" or "*qui va piano va lontano.*" I didn't understand what he was muttering, but later, when I figured it out, I was humiliated because he was telling everyone that he intended to seduce me. The others on the team that day were Bazaga, a 20-year old refugee from Franco's Spain, and a 35-year old peasant whose wife was in a mental institution. None of them had women in their lives.

As we worked the field, of course I could not keep up with them physically. And no one offered to help me. They did, however, begin threatening to rape me, using an ear of corn to make vulgar gestures. In my naïveté, I thought Angel would defend me. Instead, the other men told him he could go first.

At first I thought they were joking, but they continued to egg each other on. I began looking for a way to escape, but quickly realized I was trapped. Terror engulfed me. But someone must have been looking out for me because as their filthy talk heated up, the manager arrived on the scene. This was a man who never went out into the fields, so I don't know why he suddenly appeared three hours into our four-hour shift. Maybe he had second thoughts about sending a 14-year-old girl out with men. I think that was the case because he never again put me in a similar situation.

After the episode in the cornfield, I did not want to be seen with Angel; I did not want to have anything to do with him. Once I realized what he was after, I called him a *salaud*—roughly equivalent to dirty bastard. He responded by calling me a dirty Jew, *sale juive.* Needless to say, it hurt. This whole episode with Angel bothered me for a long time. When I left that summer to go into hiding, the villagers assumed it was because he got me pregnant.

This episode reminded me of the biblical injunction to care for and be kind to the widow and the orphan. With Kurt gone, Mama and I were unprotected and vulnerable. The lesson was not lost on me.

Since then I have come to understand the French social structure. The truth was that Angel, too, was an outcast, an outsider low on the social ladder. He was a handsome man, blond, with a little moustache, well-built and strong. But he was a foreigner and he did not own any property. The village girls would not go out with him, so he picked on me. As a hunted Jew and a foreigner, I was even lower on the social ladder than he was. Years later I found out that he never married.

In November 1942, the Germans occupied southern France—previously referred to as Free France under the puppet Vichy government—but we didn't know that because we were cut off from the outside world, without a radio or newspapers. In winter there was no farm work to be had, which reduced our meager income even further. Someone from Carcassonne told Mama a maid was needed for a young couple with a baby. I accepted the job. Upon arriving at my new job, I discovered they owned and managed a hotel in town, a hotel full of German soldiers.

I connected with one of them. He was a 16-year-old Hungarian boy who could not wait to fight for the Fuehrer. His older brother was already at the front and he was chomping at the bit to get there. He didn't even have peach fuzz on his face. Hardly older than me, I thought we both belonged in school. I felt sorry for him because he was so brainwashed. Of course I could not tell him what I thought. While I did not tell him who I was, I spoke German with him, something I should not have done. Fortunately, nothing happened.

The family I worked for struck me as unusual. Though there was plenty of water and indoor plumbing, the woman washed her infant's scalp with eau de cologne and used soap and water only on the baby's tush. And after lunch, her husband would often grab her breasts in public. I was certainly not used to that sort of thing.

I served the family meals, did laundry, especially the baby's things, and took the baby out for walks. The best part was that I had enough to eat. About four weeks after I started working there, a sweater went missing from the laundry line. The woman accused me of stealing it and I was promptly dismissed.

Back in Montlaur, Mama pleaded with the local seamstress to take me on without pay. The woman reluctantly agreed. I learned nothing, but stitched a lot of hems and sewed on many buttons.

In the meantime, my teacher from Nice, Mme. Brun, kept up a correspondence with me and sent me a few French classics for children. It was very kind of her, I thought, though they really did prove boring to me. I also attempted to amuse myself by writing a 17th century romantic play.

One evening I went out with the village girls as usual and was talking to one of the French soldiers stationed nearby when Mama came out and saw me. She smacked me across the face and went off

The old walled *cité* of Carcassonne.
The new part is in the valley outside of the walls.

in a huff. From that moment on, the soldiers stayed far away from me. When spring came, I went back to work in the fields.

During our time in Montlaur, we became friendly with one family in particular, the Duponts, who owned some land and a horse. They had two sons, Jean, 18, and Paul, who was nicknamed Popo and was my age. The family worked for others during the week and tilled their own land in the evenings and on Sundays. They had two hunting dogs that ate table scraps. The dogs would approach us while we ate and M. Dupont would kick them in the ribs to chase them away, but they always came back because they were hungry. I felt sorry for the poor animals, and felt they deserved better treatment.

Mme. Angele Dupont was a tall woman in her 40s, with a round face, red cheeks and a gentle smile. I sometimes played with Popo, who would tease me and call me *unocento* (innocent). I had trouble understanding the local dialect—it was closer to Spanish than to Italian—which had made it easier for me to understand the dialect in Nice.

Jean willingly went to Germany for the *Service de Travail Obligatoire*. This work service was mandatory for 18-year-olds in all German-occupied territories. With the Germans fighting a war on two fronts, there was a pronounced labor shortage and so, in the typical Nazi way, they began taking people as slave laborers. Many young Frenchmen in other parts of France refused to go to Germany and instead joined the *Maquis*, the French resistance.

The young men in Montlaur, like Jean, went to their service without protest. Had there been a *Maquis* in Montlaur, Kurt might have joined them. But there was nothing of the sort. After two years with the Germans, Jean returned and became the manager of the local cooperative. After the war he married Mathilde, the daughter of the manager at the *Chateau.*

During the long cold winter months Mama and I often went to the Duponts after dinner. There, in the warmth of the fire fed by the slow burning trunks of the grapevines, we would sit in the dark and talk in the glow from the hearth. Many times we got too close to the fire and our blood vessels would show through the skin of our legs. The story went that if you did that too often, your legs would become permanently "marbled."

The Noyes family (pronounced nwa-yes) was the wealthiest family in the village after the Niermans. M. Noyes was an *Ingénieur Agronome.* He had a university diploma in agricultural engineering and managed his own estate, where he had a large garden and raised fruits and vegetables for sale. I went there to buy food. They had two sons, Jean, who was bright, went into electronics and landed a job with IBM-France. He eventually married a girl from a well-to-do family from a nearby village.

His brother was slower, perhaps because of a case of childhood measles. He married a village girl with little education and Mme. Noyes used to complain that her daughter-in-law linked the *s* in *les haricots* to the *h*, a *faux pas*. (But after all, it was just string beans!) The Noyeses were good Catholics, and on Sundays madame, an attractive, elegant woman, often went to church twice, at 7 A.M. and again to major mass at 11. The village gossips said she did it to show off her outfits. The family had a full-time maid, Jeanne, who raised the boys and was very devoted to the family. I once watched her stuff some geese, a sight that can cure people from ever eating *pâté de foie gras*.

When it was decided that I had to go into hiding, Mama had to raise money for a bus ticket to Carcassonne and to give me a little pocket money. We had no money and not much left to sell. Mama had worked for years on embroidering a petit-point evening purse, and I had watched her in Vienna as she recreated a 17th century Gobelin design on the canvas that became the elegant purse. Of course, she'd never used it. Now, she took that purse to Mme. Noyes, who bought it from her for a song, but it was enough money to get me to Carcassonne.

When we lived in Montlaur, Papa was a prisoner in Rivesaltes, the French concentration camp near Perpignan. He was transferred there after a year in Gurs, while Mama continued with her efforts to liberate him. But it was a Kafkaesque world, where we filled out forms, registering our names and buying stamps for the papers (*papier timbré*). Years later I found out that the order to liberate Papa was in the office of the French camp commander, but the Vichy government forbade the release of any camp inmate at the behest of Berlin, where "the final solution of the Jewish problem" was being implemented.

By the summer of 1942, Papa was spending most of his time in the camp infirmary. He suffered from dysentery and had high blood pressure. Papa was seen by two medical commissions who declared him unfit to work. But the third commission said he was fit and on September 11, 1942 Papa was deported from Drancy north of the demarcation line to "destination unknown," Auschwitz. As the train that took him to that death factory passed Carcassonne, Papa's last postcard to us said he was wearing a bitter smile, for he imagined his

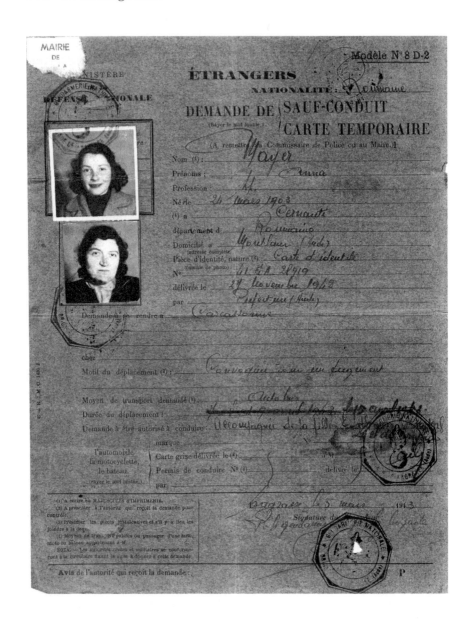

Request for a safe-conduct to Carcassonne.
March 5, 1943.

arrival in Carcassonne differently. Since he believed the German lie about resettlement to the east, he wrote that he hoped we would soon join him and be reunited.

After the war, Mama and I went back to Montlaur several times and kept in touch with some neighbors, especially with the Duponts. As the last address Papa and Kurt had known, Mama made sure that the post office always had a forwarding address in the vain hope that they survived.

I went back there with my husband Steve and again with my daughters Emily and Louise. By then Popo was married and living in a nicer house on the Grand'rue than the one he grew up in. After the war, the streets were paved, water was brought to the village from the Pyrénées, and there was indoor plumbing. The banks of the stream were covered with cement and a little canal was left in the middle for the trickle of water during the dry season. The village population had decreased to 650 and I would not be surprised if today it is smaller still.

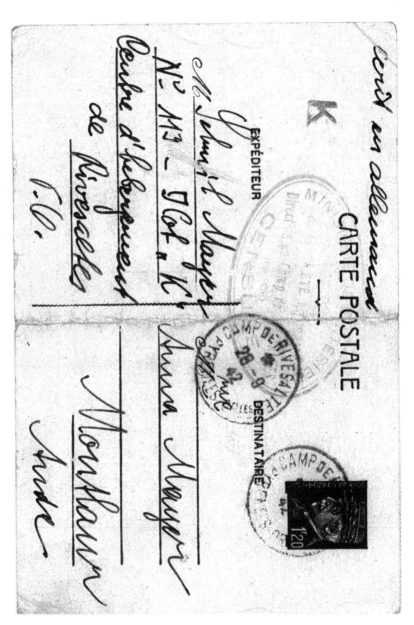

My father's last postcard, September 3, 1942.

Camp de Rivesaltes 3/9/42

Teuerstes geliebtes Muierl!

Soeben werde ich von hier nach Deutschland verladen und ich sende Euch von hier ein herzliches Lebewohl!

Bleibt gesund Alle meine Geliebten. Gott gebe, dass wir uns sehr bald irgendwo immer treffen, um unser Los miteinander zu teilen. Wir alle zusammen.

Rege Dich nicht auf. Es ist Gottesfügung. Denke an mich und behalte mich lieb. Ich küsse Dich und die Kinder. Dein und Euer Papa Adolf

My father's last postcard:

Camp of Rivesaltes, September 3, 1942
Dearest, beloved Annerl,

At this moment we are being shipped to Germany and I am sending you from here an affectionate good-bye.

Be well, all my loved ones. May God allow that we will all meet very soon somewhere so as to share our fate together, just as long as we are together. Don't get angry. It is the will of God.
Think of me and keep loving me.
I kiss you and the dear children,
your Papa Adolf.
Be blessed. Amen

/Translated from the German/ emc
My father was deported from Drancy to Auschwitz on 9/11/1942.

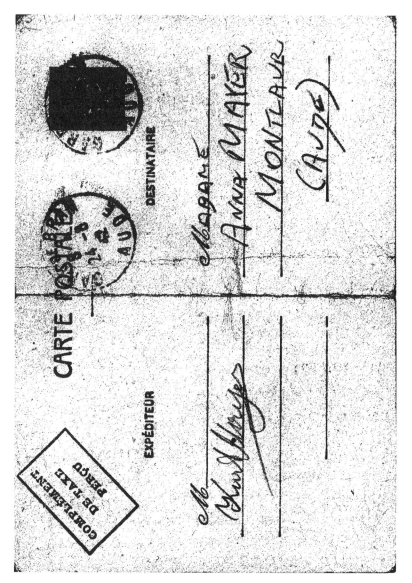

My brother Kurt's last postcard, August 23, 1942.

Kurt's last postcard,
August 23, 1942

Bram, August 23, 1942

Dear Mama,
I don't know whether this card will still reach you in Montlaur,
I hope, however, that you will be notified in time.
All of our military gear, including our blankets, had to be returned.

Tomorrow morning we are leaving for an area occupied by
Germany via (the camp of) Rivesaltes.
I paid Mr. H (what I owed him).
Otherwise I don't have much to say.
Be well and hopefully we will see each other again in peace.

Loving greetings and kisses from your Kurt.

Dear Edith, I want to kiss you too one more time.
Your brother Kurt.

Kurt's last postcard.
Translated from the German/emc
My brother was deported from Drancy to Auschwitz on 8/31/1942.

THE CONVENT IN CASTELNAUDARY

In the fall of 1942, after the mass deportations from France began, I was out working in the fields on the day Mama was contacted by a member of the Jewish underground, the *Sixième*, a code name given to the clandestine branch of the *Eclaireurs Israélites de France* (EIF, the Jewish Scouts of France). They wanted to put me into hiding. Mama's initial reaction was to say no. The messenger bluntly told her that if I were arrested or if someone in the village denounced me, I would be sent to a concentration camp and might be sexually abused by German soldiers.

My reaction to the idea of going into hiding was to say no as well, but when I was told what the possible consequences of an arrest would be, I decided to go. Given the way I was raised, sexual abuse would have been a fate worse than death for me.

For a long time I wondered how the underground found us. How did they know who we were and where we were? We certainly had not registered with any Jewish organization in Carcassonne or elsewhere, although in Montlaur everyone knew we were Jews.

I think I solved the mystery a few years ago, when I discovered that inmates in French concentration camps were told to give the authorities the names and addresses of family members on the outside so that the Nazis could "reunite families." It was one way the diabolical fiction of "resettlement in the East" was maintained.

There were two social workers in Rivesaltes, where Papa was held. One was Jewish, the other not. They knew about the reunification sham and the death camps. They told the prisoners not to give information about their families to the authorities, and they collected the names, instead. I think my father may have given them our names and that is how I was found and saved. Years later, I met Simone Weil-Lipman, the Jewish social worker from Rivesaltes. She was a lovely lady in her 80s, who explained to me how things worked in those dark days.

In any case, about nine months after our initial contact with the *Sixième*, we were notified that a hiding place had been found for me. It was time to leave Montlaur. I don't remember how they contacted us, since there were no telephones and mail was censored. I was told to appear with my belongings at an address in Carcassonne on a certain day. I needed a *sauf-conduit*, a safe conduct pass, to travel, my pretext being that I had to see a dentist.

I knew Carcassonne well, so finding my contact was no problem. When I got there, my official papers were taken from me and destroyed. Edith Mayer disappeared. I was given a new name, Elise Maillet, with papers to match, and was asked to memorize my new "story," a fiction I could easily maintain. My story was that my mother lived in Nice, my father was a POW, and I had no siblings. My parents were non-practicing Catholics, not uncommon in France.

I never forgot the date. It was July 3, 1943, two weeks after my 15th birthday. Soon after I got my papers and my story straight, a member of the Jewish resistance and I boarded a train for Castelnaudary. It was a nearby town of about 3,000 people, where a convent was located. As we waited in the station, he offered to buy me a book of my choice. To his surprise, I chose the Greek classic, *Pericles*. As we traveled, I took out my new papers and examined them. That's when I noticed my thumb print was missing, a dangerous business. My guide quickly took out his fountain pen, and I put my thumb on the inkblot he created. Then I pressed my thumb onto the false document. My papers were then "officially" complete.

I was fully aware of the dangers and was charged with adrenaline. I was petrified because I knew that my life was now in my own hands. I would have to lie constantly so as not to give myself away. In French schools there is roll call every morning and I remember being afraid that I would not react properly when my new name was called.

To make matters worse, I was anything but self-reliant. I had never been separated from Mama, not even for a sleepover at a friend's house or camp experience, and I was utterly dependent on her. I knew absolutely nothing about Catholicism, even though I had always lived in Catholic countries. Since I never had anything but the most superficial contact with non-Jews, I wondered what they were like. Needless to say, all this inexperience added to my stress.

We arrived in Castelnaudary that same afternoon. It was a very hot summer day and I remember the long walk as I carried my suitcase up a steep hill from the train station to the convent. My guide left me at the convent door and I began my new life as just another Catholic high school student. The nuns were running a vocational high school with a commercial curriculum and a home economics track.

The nuns who were running the convent school had their own hierarchy consisting of Mothers and Sisters. The Mothers were from upper middle class families, had a good education, and usually brought a dowry with them to the convent. They served as both teachers and administrators. The Sisters were from peasant and blue-collar backgrounds and had less education. They did all the hard work and drudgery: laundry, cooking, cleaning, and taking care of the rabbits and the chickens.

I stayed at the convent through the summer and so got to know some of the nuns. I discovered that nuns were not perfect—they were people just like the rest of us, with foibles and egos, tempers and attitudes. And I remember thinking that the Sisters were often much kinder than the Mothers.

I shared a room with four other girls. One of them, Naomi Zoe, was teased a lot because she was awkward and had a funny name. It wasn't vicious teasing, but it was constant and I was almost glad of that, as it deflected attention from me. I was trying hard to blend in and was careful to observe the other girls and imitate whatever they did when they prayed or crossed themselves. We took our meals in the large refectory and one of the nuns read inspirational literature to us while we ate.

On my first Sunday at the convent, I noticed that there were fewer girls at breakfast. I automatically assumed they were allowed to sleep in because it was Sunday. After breakfast I went to church with all the students. I followed them to the altar and took communion, carefully mimicking their gestures—the folded hands, the downcast and pious look upon returning from communion, the silent prayer while kneeling at my bench.

Imagine my surprise when, upon returning from church, I was greeted with dismay. Apparently, I had committed a mortal sin. I wondered how I had given myself away after only a few days. My sin was that I had eaten breakfast before taking communion, and you were not supposed to do that. (The church has since changed the rules and now you are allowed to eat before communion.) At the time I thought mortal sins should refer to major misconduct and murder, not to eating breakfast before communion!

My action provoked an uproar with both the nuns and the girls. The nuns asked me if I had had my first communion. Of course I did not. Was I baptized? I said I didn't know. So the good nuns took it upon themselves to write to the priest in the village where I was supposedly born. The reply came two months later, and, of course, there was no record of me. Then the nuns asked me if I would be willing to take catechism. I said yes, all the while crossing my fingers mentally. I was prepared to do what I had to in order to survive. I was scheduled to start the catechism in September, with the new school year.

At the same time I was hoping that the Mother Superior would put a stop to these investigations and interrogations, because I thought she knew who I was. I had been told the Mother Superior knew I was Jewish. Now I wonder if she was really aware of that. Perhaps the nuns, in their zeal, failed to tell her that they were writing to the village priest, an action that could have revealed my true identity. They may also have been attempting to convert me in order to "save my soul."

Survival was a full time job. I was constantly on my guard and had to screen every gesture, every utterance I made. I worried about giving myself away in my sleep. I had to be in the present at all times, to remember yesterday's lies and always be conscious of what I was saying or doing. As for the Catholic teachings, I had no leisure to evaluate what I learned. That had to wait until later, when the war was over.

There was just one month left to the school year when I arrived and I was put into the home economics curriculum that normally attracted the less able students. We studied a little bit of literature and some arithmetic, easy stuff. I think I read Moliere's *Bourgeois Gentilhomme* while there, at least parts of it. But again, school turned into a waste of time.

When summer vacation began, I was asked if I would be willing to stay in the convent and work. Since I had no place to go, I accepted. I shared a room with another girl who also volunteered to stay and work, but she went home every weekend. I think her name was Catherine. She had an oval face with a pointed chin, long brown hair and a lock above her forehead as was the fashion. Catherine was a gentle soul, but not once during those two months did I confide in

The convent school in Castelnaudary, my first hiding place. I'm in the front row, left. Age 15, in July 1943. This is the picture that gave me away. Catherine is in the middle row, fifth from the right. Naomi Zoe is in the back row, third from right

her in any way, tell her who I really was, how I felt, or what was on my mind. And she didn't ask any questions.

During the summer, the nuns ran a day camp for pre-schoolers. After the children arrived in the late morning, we fed them lunch, which consisted of a porridge cooked outdoors in two huge iron kettles. It was my job to clean those kettles every morning. It was hard work, because the kettles were almost bigger than I was and were very heavy. The worst of it was that the food had worms in it. You learned not to eat the hot cereal by the spoonful—you had to pick through it. After my initial revulsion, I learned to set the worms aside and eat the rest.

After lunch we took the children for walks to the grassy banks of the nearby Canal du Midi, where we let them rest for a while before playing with them. Though the weather was very hot, there was no pool or water play of any kind and there was no playground equipment. We played games, taught them songs and, after a few hours, walked them back to the convent, where they were picked up and taken home.

I enjoyed working with the children. I was in charge of lining them up in rows before walking to and from the canal, and I vividly remember one little girl who always refused to get in line when it came time to go home. She was one of the youngest in the group and would throw temper tantrums whenever it was time to leave. She would throw herself on the ground, kicking and screaming. I would pick her up and usually managed to get her to comply. On this particular day, try as I might, I could not get her to cooperate. In desperation I spanked her by slapping her on her thigh. This attracted the attention of Mother Marie-Rose, a tall, bespectacled, slender and rather young woman with aristocratic airs. She called me aside and gave me such a tongue lashing that I began to cry. That did not stop her. Instead, she added: "It's good that you should cry" and she continued to lay into me. The irony was that neither she nor the other nuns ever helped me with this child. It was always up to me to get this little girl to walk back.

Now that I am an experienced parent and know more about children, I realize that this little girl was a battered child. She was always disheveled and badly dressed, often dirty and infested with live lice. Lice are easy to kill even if eggs, or nits, are not. So lice in children were not uncommon, but live ones were. The question I ask myself now is why did the nuns at the convent not realize what the child was going through? She only threw her tantrums when it was time to go home.

When Catherine went home for the weekends, I worked with one of the Sisters on Saturdays, cleaning out the rabbit hutches and cutting branches from the weeping willows for the rabbits to eat.

Though I never confided in her, she was more outspoken about the war and gave vent to her anti-German feelings. As a result of her simple kindness and honesty, I felt closer to her than to any of the other members of the convent.

Toward the end of the summer the nuns allowed me to go out with some of the other girls. We went down to the canal where there were tippy little boats called *périssoires* for rent. They were made of wood and were less stable than canoes. We dared each other to paddle across the canal. Two of us climbed into one of these boats and, of course, capsized. Since I knew how to swim, I swam across the canal, fully clothed. I had to sneak back into the convent dripping wet. It would have been a funny story to tell, but the canal was polluted and a few weeks later I suffered the dire consequences.

Soon after that, as school was about to start, word came that I had been "burned." One of the students at the convent had relatives in Montlaur and when she went home for vacation she showed the class photo to her relatives. The person from Montlaur recognized me and told her my name was Edith Mayer, not Elise Maillet. My identity was now revealed and I had to leave the convent.

I was gone the very next day.

MOISSAC
In the Hospital

In the rush to get me out of Castelnaudary, there was no time to find another suitable hiding place so I was sent to Moissac, where there was a home for Jewish children. Some of their parents had been deported; others were languishing in French concentration camps, and some of the children were there because they were shipped out of Germany or Austria on a *Kindertransport*. The home was run by the *Sixième* under cover of the EIF, a legal organization under Vichy. The plan was to send me to work for two weeks to help with harvests. After that, schools would open and I would be placed in one of them.

The children's home was relatively full, though plans were underway to find hiding places for everyone because it was too dangerous to keep us together. The *Sixième* had learned the lesson of the home in Isieu, where 42 children were denounced and deported to Auschwitz by the infamous Klaus Barbie, the butcher of Lyon.

It was harder to hide children who did not speak French or those who spoke with a German accent. The leaders told the German children to say they were from Alsace-Lorraine, a region in France where German was spoken. I was fortunate because I spoke French like a native and linguistically I could pass. I watched the other children in Moissac memorize their "stories" as they got ready to leave.

I arrived in Moissac on a Friday. That evening, one of the counselors, two other teenagers and I went to the movies. When we came back, I went to bed feeling tired and woke up the next day with a painful sore throat. I could not swallow, was running a high fever and was feeling utterly miserable. I was taken to the hospital where I was diagnosed with diphtheria. The people who ran the home were extremely concerned because the children were about to be sent into hiding and could not afford to get sick. They nicknamed me *la pestiférée*, or the plague-ridden one, and my room was fumigated.

At the hospital I was injected with horse serum, then the standard treatment for diphtheria. The serum caused unbearable itching that could only be relieved with the occasional application of talcum powder, but even that was not much help. I also remember getting the inside of my throat daubed with some kind of blue medication to relieve the pain and reduce the swelling. (I think it was gentian violet.) But swallowing remained painful and I was feeling very sick.

To prevent others from contracting the disease, the doctors placed me in the hospital pavilion for contagious diseases. A woman in her 30s in the room next door had scarlet fever. We shared the same nurse. After four weeks in that room, I was still contagious but starting to feel better when I came down with scarlet fever. At that point I was convinced I was going to die, that there was no point in continuing to hang on to life. I felt we were all going to die sooner or later, and I wanted to die with my Mama instead of alone like a dog. I wanted to go back to Montlaur so we could die together. I wrote all of this in a letter to my mother. Since I had no stationery, I wrote on toilet paper and handed it to one of the *résistants* who would get it to my mother through the usual circuitous method.

The *Sixième* had worked out a system. With mail censorship it was too dangerous to send letters through the post office. So to communicate with my mother, I would give my letter to a *résistant* who would give it to another, and so on until someone would personally hand her my letter. Her mail to me was handled in the same manner. (I broke the rule only once, in March 1944, when I wrote my mother a poem for her birthday. I dropped it in a mailbox without putting a return address on the envelope.)

There I was in the hospital in Moissac, sick as a dog, depressed, with all the fight gone out of me. I couldn't take it anymore and I was ready to give up. The doctor who examined me said I was run down and malnourished. Because the hospital food was inadequate, the people at the children's home decided to supplement my diet with their own food. Twice a day they sent two children to bring me food. It wasn't much better than the food the hospital was giving me, but I was hungry and it allowed me to be a bit more selective (I hated rutabagas, for example, so if the home sent chestnuts I could eat them instead.) We got a lot of cabbage, rutabagas, turnips, onions and celery.

Because it was harvest time, the home sent chestnuts, persimmons and a little protein food. I learned to eat larger quantities in order to get more nourishment even though it wasn't good for my waistline. After four more weeks in the hospital, I recovered.

While I was there, the lice in my hair and scalp multiplied and thrived. I was too ashamed to tell the nurse that I had lice but when I came down with scarlet fever and had at least another four-week stay in the hospital, I decided to tell the nurse. Lice fell out of my head whenever I ran a comb through my hair. Did you know lice bite? The nurse applied a medication that killed the live ones, and did it more than once. I had started out with fashionably long hair in the style of Rita Hayworth and Veronica Lake, but after I left the hospital I got myself a very short haircut.

While I was getting better, I was also very bored. The nurse was kind enough to bring me materials to make myself a little tote bag. She dyed some old sheets a bright red and brought me a large piece of cardboard. I cut it up and sewed the red fabric over the cardboard, using the additional fabric for the gussets and the handle. The bag turned out to be a very useful piece of luggage when I crossed into Switzerland in late spring 1944.

I finally left the hospital in November. It was cold, and I was shivering. When I got to the home, I discovered it was almost deserted with only a few children left. I shared a bedroom with one or two other girls. Because we did not have enough blankets to keep ourselves warm, we took spare mattresses and used them as blankets to keep out the chill.

After a few days in the home, I was sent off to my next hiding place, the Lycée de Jeunes Filles in Mende, department of the Lozère, in the Massif Central, approximately 200 miles northeast of Moissac.

MENDE AND THE ENGLISH TEACHER

It was mid-November and the weather was miserable. I began to doubt my own survival and, worse, I was losing the will to fight and to resist. Death was all around us and it seemed like just a matter of time before I, too, would get caught in the dragnet and be killed. It was the lowest point in my life.

I traveled to Mende by train with Toubib, a female *résistant*. At one point the door to our compartment opened and two men came in and asked for our papers. We produced our false identity cards; I was gripped by fear. One man, who seemed pleasant and polite, handled the procedure. He was tall and wore a gray overcoat. The other one supervised and seemed to be the more menacing of the two. He was tall and wore a dark winter coat. As they inspected our cards, the man in the gray coat noticed that the cards were issued by the same town of Orange. Suddenly suspicious, the inspector asked, "Are you related?" Thinking quickly, Toubib replied, "Yes, she is my niece." With that, the ID cards were politely returned to us.

Hiding under a false identity was not a simple matter. I was still not used to being on my own. Worse than that was the constant lying. I had to be on my guard at all times. Every word, every gesture had to be controlled and scrutinized to see whether it was safe. This created a constant state of tension and pressure that escalated with each passing day. It also created incredible loneliness, since I could not share my thoughts with anyone. I couldn't even keep a journal; it was out of the question. If someone would find my notes, it would put me and everyone around me at risk.

In this frame of mind, I was sent to the huge *lycée*/boarding school in Mende. The building was cold, gray and, like all French *lycées*, it was forbidding and prison-like. The school had an iron gate and a fence with wrought iron spikes. As a boarder I was not allowed to leave the premises, except for group outings—like the weekly trip to the public showers and the customary Sunday afternoon walk. Only an authorized person was allowed to sign me out.

Unlike my stay in Castelnaudary, I was not alone in this untenable situation. There were 12 other Jewish girls in this school. They were placed there by the clandestine branch of the OSE, a Jewish organization focused on saving children, and by the *Sixième*. I recognized one of the girls from my brief stay in Moissac, and soon knew all 12 girls. And though we knew it was dangerous to stick together, we still tended to seek each other out. There was some comfort in being able to speak openly, even if we had to use code language. Apples were Germans, pears were Poles.

The huge dormitory may have housed as many as 40 girls. The beds were lined up in two rows against the walls. They had iron headboards and small night tables, where we put most of our possessions. The room was dimly lit, unheated and drab, just like the rest of the place, and it was most uncomfortable.

Classwork was a disaster for me. I arrived at school six weeks into the semester and had no textbooks. In French secondary schools textbooks, school supplies and art materials have to be purchased by the students. The *Sixième* was too busy saving lives to worry about providing their charges with textbooks, so my grades suffered. I began to think of myself as stupid and convinced myself I had a mental block for math when I saw my tests come back covered in red ink.

And then the English teacher appeared. At first she was just one of my many teachers. She was young, dark-haired, rather tall, slender and well groomed. I thought she was pretty. After a few days, she gave me a textbook. Then she helped me with the chapters I had missed and checked my homework. Thanks to her efforts, I caught up with the rest of the class rather quickly and soon received good grades. English became the only subject where I earned very good grades.

I do not remember this young woman's name other than her initials on my report card, SL. When I realized that she was taking a special interest in me, I asked the other girls whether it was safe to trust her. They said that was fine. I never told Mademoiselle L. who I was and she never asked me any direct questions, but I am convinced that she somehow figured out which girls were in hiding.

One day she asked me whether I had a winter coat and warm socks. I was flabbergasted. No one had ever asked me anything about my own needs, not even the nuns or the Mother Superior at the convent, who surely knew who I was. I almost burst into tears as she gave me some yarn and knitting needles so I could knit myself some socks.

She also asked me if I would like to become a girl scout. I accepted enthusiastically. I went to meetings held in a remote corner of the *lycée*, studied my scout manual and prepared for my "Promise." I appreciated the break in the drab routine and liked the scout values and ideals, since they complemented and reinforced my own.

I had only spent a month with the group when, just before Christmas vacation, suspecting that I would not return, Mademoiselle L. asked whether I wanted to make my Girl Scout Promise before I left. I accepted joyfully and became an official girl scout in record time.

The high point of my stay in Mende came when Mademoiselle L. invited me to her house. Even though it was just for a few hours, it was so nice to be in a home that was comfortable and warm, that had real furniture. It was so nice to be away from the institution. But above all it was such a privilege to be with someone I looked up to and who took an interest in me. Mademoiselle treated me to a *goûter*, the customary French mid-afternoon snack. Afterward, we spoke at length. She asked me whether my mother had explained the facts of life to me. By then I was 15 and a half and I told her I knew something about it. Before I left that afternoon, she wrote a little something into my memory book:

Que seulement je fasse de ma vie une flûte simple et droite
Pareille à un roseau que l'on puisse emplir de musique.

(May I make of my life a flute, simple and straight,
     Like a reed that can be filled with music.)

It was a line from the Indian poet, Rabindranath Tagore. I took it to heart and never forgot it.

Christmas vacation came and soon it was time for me to leave. I never saw Mademoiselle L. again, but we did correspond after the war.

One day in May 1944, five months later, while I was still in hiding, still struggling to stay alive and not be found out, something dawned on me. This unassuming English teacher had something other people did not have. I did not know what it was, but whatever it was I wanted to have it too. It had to be powerful, for this woman acted like no one else. She cared, she took risks, and showed compassion. She went beyond the role of teacher. She radiated light amidst all the darkness. Where did she get her courage, her strength, her character? She did it all so simply, with humility, without affectation or grandiose manners. I didn't know what it was, but there was no one to answer my burning questions and I had to wait years before figuring it out by myself.

I did not realize it then but that day in May 1944 was a turning point for me. It was the beginning of my awakening to the life of the spirit. That day I realized I had ambition: I wanted to make something of my life. I didn't want to stay down in the dumps. I wasn't sure I would do anything great, but I knew I wanted to be somebody. I did not want to remain ignorant and unskilled.

After the war I wrote to Mademoiselle L. and told her that I was going to try to catch up with my education and prepare for the *Baccalauréat*. She was very supportive and thought that I could do it, though almost no one else did. She also told me she had applied for a transfer to Caen, a city in Normandy that had been heavily damaged during the Allied landings. That was just like her. She knew there would be much work to do, much need for healing the physical and emotional scars of the war. After she moved I lost track of her. Even so, though I had known her for only five weeks, she remained an inspiration and a role model for the rest of my life.

FLORAC
The Christmas Camp

It was 1944 and Christmas vacation time. Staying in school was out of the question as the schools closed for the holidays, but the children in hiding could not go home. So the *Sixième* organized a scout camp. They housed us in unused military barracks in the small town of Florac, in the Massif Central Mountains of France.

I arrived in Florac on a cold, dark December night, shivering and wondering whether I would ever be warm again. Gradually other people began to trickle in as I waited in the dark, shoulders hunched, freezing. One of the fellows asked me if I knew how to dance the *hora*, a Zionist folk dance. I said I didn't, so he offered to teach me. We formed a circle as others joined us, and those who knew the songs sang and danced at the same time. Soon, everyone was dancing and we warmed up quickly. This set the tone for the next two weeks, a wonderful time under the loving direction and watchful eye of the *Sixième*.

The wooden barracks we were directed to, however, offered no relief from the bitter cold. Though there was a wood-burning stove in the middle of each, the walls had no insulation. With 20 people to a barrack, we were assigned bunk-beds, four to a section, with two bunks on the bottom and two bunks on top. There were mattresses and rather drab blankets. At the far end of the camp was a cement building that contained the toilets and the showers, forcing us to cross the length of the camp to get there. During the day this presented no problem, but at night, if nature called, we would leave the barrack, turn the corner and relieve ourselves in the open. Everyone did that except a 12-year-old girl from Germany, we shall call her K., who simply refused to go out in the cold. The first night she wet her bed, so after that we made sure that she slept on a bottom bunk. K. was soft-spoken, with olive skin, regular features, a gentle smile, shoulder-length black hair and puppy eyes.

The incredible thing about our stay at the camp was that there was plenty of food. I have no idea how they managed it! We had lots of potatoes—we all helped peel them—and got some protein as well. I don't recall going hungry.

We were about 80 people at the camp, mostly children, in the care of our valiant saviors. I'd met several of the adults because whenever I was transferred from one hiding place to another someone had to accompany me. While I was in hiding, some of them had visited and brought me letters from Mama.

During our stay, the camp was always busy. Our day started with roll call, a salute to the French flag, calisthenics and kitchen duties. We went on hikes, played dodge ball (*ballon prisonnier*) and sang lots of songs. We were told to organize ourselves into troops by age, choose a mascot and motto, and write theme songs. Each day every troop presented its colors and motto.

I still remember our troop's song. We chose the *cabri*, the mountain goat, as our mascot. Our motto was *Tiens bon!* (Hang in there!) I still remember the theme song's refrain:

> *Sur les monts comme dans la vie*
> *Disons-nous je suis un cabri*
> *Difficultés nous franchirons*
> *Grâce à notre devise: Tiens bon!*

(On the mountains, as in life, let us tell ourselves that
we are mountain goats. Difficulties we will overcome,
thanks to our motto: *Tiens bon!*)

I remember the older boys' motto because I liked it. It was "*On les aura!*" (We will get them!) yelled out loud, and the echoing answer was "*On les a eus!*" (We got them!)

My four weeks of scout training in Mende had prepared me well for this experience. Each troop produced skits for our mutual entertainment, ranging from tame stories, like "The three little kittens who lost their mittens" to political satires and biting comedies.

On both Friday nights we had *Oneg Shabbats*, where I learned many of the Hebrew songs I know. We made *Kiddush* (the sanctification of the wine) did the *benchen* (grace after meals) and sang *zemirot* (*Shabbat* hymns) to our heart's content. We were way out in the hinterlands so no one could hear us, but I wondered about it at the time. Recently I found out that our counselors took turns standing guard around the camp to make sure outsiders did not come in.

The counselors also tried to be surrogate parents. They organized talks about love and friendship for those of us who were 17 or older, and I was annoyed to be told I was too young to attend.

When we first got to the scout camp we were eager to share our experiences and felt free to tell each other our real names and where we came from. Very quickly our leaders cautioned us not to give out too much information to each other because, if we were caught and tortured, we might give each other away. We learned to limit ourselves to sharing feelings and thoughts, but we refrained from giving out possibly compromising information.

We called our leaders chieftains and used their scout nicknames. Giraffe was young and tall and, of course, he had a long neck. Vishnu, named for an Indian deity, was a woman who had escorted me from one hiding place to another. Chameau (the camel) (Frederic Shimon Hammel) was much older than the others, and later I found out that he was a founding member of the *Sixième*. Eventually, he went to Israel and wrote a book called *Remember Amalek*. Chef Pierron was in charge. He was young, about 25, and handsome. We found out that he was engaged to be married.

Toward the end of our time in the camp, the chieftains wrote a song summarizing many of our activities. This was the refrain:

> *Nous sommes cent synthétiques*
> *Qui campons tous à Florac*
> *Dans un camp a-spécifique*
> *Bien planqués dans des baraques.*

(We are one hundred fakes [synthetics]
Camping in Florac
In a nonspecific camp,
Well-hidden in barracks).

I remember that, at the time, I did not know the meaning of the words synthetic and nonspecific.

The chieftains admirably succeeded in what they had set out to do. They provided us with a much needed psychological and physical

Le Camp de Florac: The girls. I'm in the front, second from right in my gray Tyrolian Janker with the green lapels.

Souris is standing on the left; Giraffe is behind him; Jacques Majerholc, standing, fourth from left; Chef Pierron standing on the right.

break from the difficult and frightening days in hiding. We had plenty to eat and a chance to be normal. Above all, they succeeded in boosting our morale.

As a result of the program, I was *"gonflée à bloc,"* pumped to the max, and revitalized, ready to fight for my survival. Before I left, I was called in to see Chef Pierron. Naturally, I wondered what I had done wrong and expected to be bawled out. Instead, Chef Pierron pulled out the desperate and depressing letter to my mother written on toilet paper while I was in the hospital. In it I had expressed the desire to go back to Montlaur because I couldn't take it any more, because we were all going to die anyway and I preferred to die with her. Chef Pierron told me he had taken the liberty of reading the letter and never gave it to my mother because he thought it would make her sad. Now he asked me if I wanted him to transmit it to her. By the time he finished talking to me I was in tears. I tore up the letter and wrote her a much happier missive.

I searched for Chef Pierron for many years after the war and did not learn his real name until Frida Wattenberg wrote a book in 2004 about the Jewish Resistance in France. In it I found the wartime code names and real names of our Jewish chieftains. Chef Pierron's real name was Roger Klimovitsky, and Climaud, a dimunitive of his last name, was his false name. He was arrested after D-Day, tortured and deported to Auschwitz. He came back to Paris, physically wounded, but emotionally strong. He later married his sweetheart. They had three children and those of us from the group who could visited him in Paris and provided lots of support. He died in 2000 before I had the chance to personally thank him. His name is inscribed on the walls of the Paris Holocaust Memorial. In October 2004, during a visit to France, I paid my respects at his gravesite.

My Christmas vacation flew by quickly and soon came word that the *Sixième* was sending me to another boarding school in Pezenas. It turned out to be the worst hiding place for me and I would not have survived if I hadn't been reinvigorated emotionally by my wonderful experiences in Florac.

PEZENAS

Pezenas is a town about half-way between Montpellier and Beziers. The school there served mainly students from the surrounding rural area and though almost all the girls boarded during the week, they went home every Sunday and often on Thursdays as well. (There was no school on Thursdays in those days.) The place was not geared to someone like me, who depended entirely on school for basics. There was no shower room, no laundry, and not much food.

The school was a *lycée* that went up to the *troisième* form (equivalent to the ninth grade). If the course was completed, students could take the exam for their *Brevet Elémentaire*. If the students wanted to continue for the *Baccalauréat*, requiring three more years of schooling, they had to transfer to a regular *lycée*.

In Castelnaudary and Mende we were taken every week to the public baths for our showers. In Pezenas, the girls went home to bathe while I remained dirty; the school authorities wouldn't allow me to use the washroom when no one was around. We were only able to wash our hands and face and brush our teeth during scheduled times and under staff supervision. I couldn't wash my hair or my private parts. When I had to present my comb for inspection, I wiped it on the only towel I had. I wasn't given linen to sleep on and was loaned a scratchy blanket by another student. The school wouldn't even provide me with sheets. Yet the school required that our clothes be neatly folded on a shelf next to our beds. Initially, my clothes were clean but not ironed, so folding them neatly was difficult. Eventually, all my clothes became dirty, and so was I because the school would not allow me to do anything about my hygiene. I was not given the opportunity to wash myself or my clothing and this became embarrassing, especially in front of my classmates.

A word here about clothes. In Montlaur, I had outgrown all the clothes I had brought from Nice. Taking two of my dresses, I made them into blouses. I also converted a pair of my brother's pants into a skirt. I think I had a sweater my mother had knitted and a threadbare coat. I had two pairs of panties, two pairs of socks and a bra. I wore these same clothes every day for a couple of years.

I had gotten my first menstrual period when I was 14 years and three months old. Blessedly, I only got it twice, and then it stopped for four years because of malnutrition. Imagine if I had had to cope with that when I wasn't able to wash myself at all!

The worst part of Pezenas was hunger. The other girls would come back every week with baskets stocked with ham, sausage, cheese, bread and other food. I depended on the food the school served us. We got watery soup, two tablespoons of pasta, and once a week, a quarter of a candy bar.

During a school break I remained in the school while the other students went home. I ate with the kitchen staff and noticed that they ate very well and helped themselves to our rations. Mme. l'Econome, the woman in charge, held the keys to the larder, but I don't know what she did with our food. Years later, I ran into her in Toulouse. She recognized me and gave me such a big hello that I had trouble believing her sincerity after the way I had literally starved under her care.

In addition to the tiny quantities of food they gave us, the quality was so bad that the other girls turned their noses up at it. Every day, after meals, they would go to their baskets and eat their provisions. No one shared anything with me. One girl, who must have come from a poorer family than the others, would run out of her supplemental food by mid-week. The others shared their food with her but not with me. Eventually, my hunger pangs were so bad that the smell of food drove me crazy. I got into the habit of retreating to the toilets while the girls ate their goodies.

Classwork was a disaster. I had no textbooks. When I asked classmates to lend me one of their books, they told me that they needed them for their own homework. I got terrible grades and was never able to prepare for class because I couldn't read my assignments.

In this school I clearly stood out because I was different, lacked basic supplies, and had to stay in during weekends. Soon the girls began to spy on me. They constantly asked me if my mother had sent me any letters. I usually said yes and that I had gotten my letters days earlier. But they were watching, because they would retort: "No, you didn't." During mail call everyone could hear who got letters and my name was never called.

Then there was the *directrice*, the principal. She looked like a witch and acted like one. She was a middle-aged woman with wiry, graying hair, who usually wore a gray coat and walked around with a cane. It was January 1944 and lots of girls came down with colds and coughs. She would walk into the dining hall and demand that we stop coughing. I remember almost turning blue and red, trying to suppress a cough. Our gym teacher would work us hard, and it was harder on me because I did not have much energy. What did the *directrice* do? She yelled at the gym teacher in front of the students for working us so hard, and then had the nerve to add: "I am feeding them to do mathematics, not gym."

During the early February break, I pleaded for permission to do my laundry. This turned into a humiliating experience. The *directrice* had me put my dirty clothes out on the floor. When she saw my bra she picked it up with the tip of her cane and flung it across the room saying "You don't need that," and refused to let me wash my clothes. I could not understand her. Didn't she know who I was? Was she deliberately torturing me? I had no idea. I had been led to believe that the heads of the schools where the *Sixième* hid Jewish children always knew who they were, so the principal's behavior left me puzzled.

For more than five weeks I went without cleaning myself. My hair was dirty (no lice, thank God), my clothes were filthy, and I was hungry, cold and miserable. If not for my time in the Florac scout camp, I probably would have fallen into complete despair. Then my health began to suffer. I had a pimple on my elbow that developed into a large sore, my cold never went away and I coughed for months. I developed chilblains, too. Fortunately, in mid-February, they sent a *resistant* for me and I left Pezenas for good. I must have told her everything because they did not send me back.

That same day, she took me to a house in a village that shall always remain nameless. We arrived after dark on a very cold night, the ground covered with snow. Other girls were there, some of whom I remembered from our two weeks in Florac. On the first night I collapsed into a clean bed with clean sheets. I spent the entire next day cleaning myself up, washing my hair and doing laundry. That evening I was told that I would be leaving the following morning. I quickly ran outside where I had put my laundry out to dry and found it was frozen stiff. I took the laundry off the line and arranged the pieces around the wood stove so it would dry in time for my departure. Unfortunately, some of my things were too close to the stove and were burned. That was a small disaster since I couldn't replace what I had lost, but at least what I had left was clean! That evening the girls and I talked until late into the night, sharing confidences about our hopes and dreams for the future.

I spent only 36 hours in that house and, to this day, I do not know where I was.

CAHORS
In the Home for Retarded Girls

The next morning, I went to Cahors, another small town in the region. Like the convent in Castelnaudary, it was a vocational high school for girls with a commercial and a home economics curriculum. The physical plant was much nicer than the usual *lycée*. It had a campus with an open feeling, there was a lawn, and once a week we were taken to the public showers. I could wash my hair and do my laundry. And the staff did not steal our food like they did in Pezenas.

In Cahors there were six of us in hiding. Everyone had been placed there either by the *Sixième* or by the OSE. Because of the school's more adequate amenities and the girls I found there, it was a nicer place to be and I appreciated it, especially after Pezenas.

I was placed in the Home Economics section. There was a pleasant surprise when the school gave us fabric to make blouses in sewing class! Working with a pattern, I made myself a simple, royal blue blouse that was a much-needed addition to my wardrobe.

The school also provided each of us with textbooks. Class work was easy and not much of an academic challenge. My fellow students were much nicer than the girls in Pezenas and I became friendly with a few, though I still did not confide in anyone.

Several weeks into my stay, the idyll was over. One morning, the principal interrupted our classes and told us that the German forces requisitioned the school for use as their headquarters. We had to vacate the premises by 5 P.M. that same day. Everyone was sent packing, including the six of us in hiding. What was the principal going to do with us? There was no time to contact the underground, but our resourceful

With fellow students and a teacher in the Cahors vocational school.
(I'm in the front, bottom right.)

directrice found us a great hiding place: the nearby home for mentally retarded girls (Centre de Jeunes Filles Déficientes).

Since we were obviously not retarded, the Center left us to our own devices. We shared meals and went on outings with the others, but otherwise we were left alone. By then it was late March and the weather was becoming milder. We could sit outside and as we mended our clothes, we took turns reading aloud from the classics. One book we read was *Jocelyn* by Lamartine.

To be around retarded girls was a novel experience for all of us. There were teenage girls who could only read at early grade levels or they were learning to scrub floors. But there were also girls who had no other place to go. I remember one 15-year-old, a very nice girl whose parents were alcoholics. Social Services put her in this home for her own protection. The Center seemed something of a catch-all, and it was sad to see how normal kids were warehoused among the mentally disabled.

We spent two weeks there, until Easter, when our fearless leaders were able to place us with families for Easter vacation.

I was told not to discuss anything with my assigned family. I have no idea what they knew, but they listened to the BBC, a very dangerous thing to do. At the dinner table, they liked to tell anti-German jokes and felt free to express their political views in front of me. The best part was that there was plenty to eat, and the food was good. The worst part was getting to the indoor toilet. I had to walk through the parents' bedroom to get there, and they always slept late, so I could not "go" before 10 A.M. That was torture!

This loving couple had a 19-year-old daughter who, I was told, was engaged to be married. But she had a friend visiting—a handsome young man—and they were always kissing. That surprised me because I thought that being engaged to someone required fidelity. I did the smart thing, I said nothing and didn't ask any questions.

Someone took a picture of me during Easter week. I was wearing my famous "pants" skirt and one of the blouses I had made from a dress. I don't look skinny and I am smiling.

After Easter vacation, I was sent back to the vocational school in Cahors. The Germans decided they didn't want it after all. I stayed there for another month. Then someone from the *Sixième* picked me up and brought me to a hotel in Clermont Ferrand, a nearby town. I had learned not to ask questions and assumed that I was going to another hiding place. Unbeknownst to me, this time it was in preparation for our escape to Switzerland.

The six of us in hiding at the Centre de Jeunes Filles Déficientes in Cahors, March 1944. (I'm in the front, second from the right.)

During that year I had lived like a hunted animal, always on the run. The close calls and constant fear gave the whole year the aspect of a nightmare. So after the war, I felt the need to go back to revisit some of these places, to make sure they were real. I went back to Cahors; the school was much smaller than I remembered. I never went back to Pezenas, Florac or Mende.

In May, while still in Cahors, I wrote down some thoughts of a noncompromising nature. I recognized that Mademoiselle L., the English teacher from Mende, was different from anyone else I had known. The only other person in her league was Mme. Brun, my teacher from Nice, These women had a special quality of being. They weren't sugar-coated; they had character and were caring individuals. I wanted to know what made them that way because I wanted to be like them. They were my heroes and their moral support and faith in my ability to succeed proved invaluable to me after the war.

Because I was forced to keep things inside over such a long period of time, I developed an intense inner life and became very introspective. I also learned to control what passed my lips, even in anger. And I turned to the God of my childhood and to the prayers I had been taught to sustain me during these difficult times.

FLIGHT TO SWITZERLAND

After two or three days at the hotel in Clermont Ferrand, about 30 children were assembled. I knew some of them from Florac and from the other hiding places. But until the eve of departure, they didn't tell us why we were there. I assumed that I was being transferred to another hiding place. Soon, however, we discovered the answer: They were going to try to smuggle us over the border into Switzerland. We were told to take only what we could carry, wear two layers of underwear and extra clothes so we would have what to wear once we got to Switzerland. If we had real papers, we were to take them along.

I remember one lucky boy who sewed his papers into the lining of his coat. We were told that, if stopped, we should say that we were going on vacation, though that was an unlikely story. After all, schools were still in session in May. Nevertheless, our *resistants* gave us confidence. We didn't look like children going to camp, what with our wooden-soled shoes, our coats and hand-held bags. We were told to leave our other belongings behind—that they would keep them for us. Mama had already kept my teddy bear during all this time.

I recall that, as we packed, we did not necessarily choose the most useful items but took things with sentimental value, like photographs of our families. We were told that the Swiss accepted girls up to the age of 18 and boys up to the age of 16. A couple of the boys were 17 and so made themselves look a year younger by wearing short pants to be more convincing. Since most of us had no documents, the Swiss would be forced to take our word for everything, something they did not like to do. We were told that we were the second group of children the *Sixième* tried to send into Switzerland. The first group of 20 teenagers made it across successfully, just the week before.

That night, before we left, I wrote a poem called "Tristesse."

TRISTESSE

Que je me sens drôle ces jours-ci
Il me semble que je ne suis pas moi-même.
Le monde me parait si petit
Et je sens comme c'est doux quand on s'aime. :

Oh oui, aimer,
Ne point connaître le vilain côté de ce monde,
Mais c'est trop rêver,
Et il faut songer à l'orage, là-bas, qui gronde,

Il gronde, fort,
Il fait trembler la terre entière
Il ne ménage pas les morts
Et sème partout tellement de misère.

Orage, orage, quand t'arrêteras-tu
Afin que chaque homme sans crainte d'être pendu
Puisse exprimer librement
Jusqu'à ses plus profonds sentiments.
Moi aussi je voudrais pouvoir exprimer
Mes pensées en toute franchise
Mais je me sens comprimée
Comme dans une cage, prise.

C'est alors que ces noires idées tourbillonnent dans ma tête
Et me dépriment pour toute la journée
Je deviens méchante comme une mauvaise bête
Sans vouloir le faire exprès.

Oh papier!
Je ne veux rien te cacher..
Comme seul confident
Tu sais si bien soulager.

SADNESS

How strange I feel these days.
I don't feel like myself
The world seems so small
And I feel how sweet it is to love one another.

Oh yes, to love one another
Not to know the ugly side of this world
But that's too much of a dream
And we must remember the storm that rages over there.

It rages, loud
It makes the whole earth tremble
It causes so many deaths
And sows so much misery everywhere.

Storm, storm, when will you stop?
So that each man without fear for his life
Is free to express
Even his innermost feelings.
I too would like to be able to express
My own thoughts in freedom,
But I feel compressed
As though trapped in a cage.

That's when those black thoughts swirl in my head
And depress me for the whole day,
I become nasty like a mean beast
Without meaning to do so.

Oh paper!
I do not want to hide anything from you,
For as the only confidant,
You know how to provide relief.

(Clermont Ferrand, Vichy France
May 20, 1944
Translated from the French)

We were scheduled to leave after breakfast and take the train to the border town of St. Julien. Then we would attempt to cross the border on foot. One of our leaders would come with us. She was not one of the regulars who escorted me from one hiding place to another or hand delivered mail from my mother. Her name was Marianne. At the station in St. Julien we were to meet two paid Spanish guides (refugees from the Spanish Civil War) who supposedly knew the way through the woods.

In the morning all went as planned, that is until we got to St. Julien. It had a tiny train station and the train only stopped for three minutes, not long enough to let 30 youngsters get off. Half of us succeeded and the rest of us were stuck on the train, me included. The fear we felt grew as each turn of the wheel took us further away. Finally the train stopped and we scrambled to get off.

I always wondered why the station master had given the green light for the train to pull out. I thought he had rigidly followed the allotted three-minute schedule for that little town. Recently, I learned that in our haste, according to one of the boys in our group, we opened the train doors on the wrong side instead of on the platform side. Perhaps that's why the station master could not see that passengers were still trying to get off.

Since the road was patrolled by German soldiers, it was too dangerous to walk on the road back to St. Julien. And so, we walked back on the tracks. It took us about two hours, a veritable eternity. We had a 5-year-old with us and we had to carry our bags as well, making the trip even more difficult. Jacques Majerholc, one of the older boys, carried the 5-year-old while Paulette, the boy's older sister, carried Jacques' bag. Making matters worse, the ties on the tracks were not evenly spaced, so we had to adjust our stride with every step. To this day I cannot walk on railroad tracks without reliving that experience.

Luckily, near the train station, the rest of the group was waiting for us, crouched behind a hedge near an open field. The two guides were already there and so, without taking time to rest, we continued toward the Swiss border.

We crossed open fields by running across them one at a time, ducking all the way to avoid being seen. At one point we heard patrols marching on the road and quickly hid behind trees and shrubbery. We realized we were all at the mercy of anyone coughing, sneezing, or making a sound.

We resumed our journey once the patrol moved on. After an hour of walking, I noticed some of the packages from our group lying on the ground. Like Hansel and Gretel we had left a trail. Some of us had taken along too much stuff and could not carry it. Then our Spanish guides realized that they had literally led us around in a big circle.

We then took a different route through the underbrush. That presented a problem for the 5-year old. Several of the bigger boys took turns carrying him, but the branches were hitting him in the face and he would cry out from pain every time. So the guides assembled us and told us that they did not want to jeopardize everyone's life because of the boy. If he did not stop crying, we would have to leave him behind. None of us wanted that to happen, so we took greater care moving branches.

It had recently rained and the ground was soaked. The shoes someone had bought for me had long been falling apart. They had wooden soles and now in the mud made walking even more difficult. By midday the sun was warm and we were sweltering in our double layers of clothing as we trekked through the underbrush.

After what seemed like an eternity, we came upon two coils of barbed wire stretched along the border. They must have been six feet high. The guides brought cutters and we managed to walk through the first one. We did not talk. We were in no man's land, between the barbed wire coils, and were still not safe, for the Germans were known to pursue people into no man's land and shoot them. At least we were walking in the right direction. Soon we came to the second coil of barbed wire and beyond that we saw the Swiss side of the border, a tall fence strung straight across with barbed wire. There stood a Swiss soldier staring at us, with his gun over his shoulder. The sight of him gave us renewed energy as we crawled under or squeezed between the razor sharp wires to get to the other side.

To my deep regret and disbelief Marianne Cohn, the young woman who had accompanied us, returned to France. When she stayed on the French side of the barbed wire fence I asked her, "You are not going back to that hell, are you?" She didn't say anything, but nodded to indicate that she was indeed going back. Later, I learned that she was leading another group of 20 children to the border when she was caught, tortured and killed. All the children were saved by the intervention of the mayor of Annemasse and the Cardinal of Nice. During a recent visit to the new Museum of French Resistance in Toulouse, I stumbled upon a terrible photo of Marianne. Her mutilated and ravaged body had been found in a ditch.

Once we arrived on Swiss soil our joy was boundless. We kissed the ground, hugged each other and exchanged true names...it was an

Marianne Cohn.

overwhelming experience. I wrote a poem right then and there called "Freedom."

LIBERTE

Mon rêve est réalité
Nous voilà en liberté!
Plus de cache-cache,
Plus de mensonge,
Plus de faux papiers,
Plus rien qui me ronge.

Je ne veux point penser au lendemain.
Pour aujourd'hui nous sommes tous réunis
Et ici on ne nous veut que du bien.

Est-ce vrai que je suis libre?
Il me semble que je suis ivre!
Je me laisse aller à ce délice
Car fini est le supplice
De sans cesse jouer la comédie
Sans jamais montrer son ennui.

Mais désormais tout celà est fini
Et j'aspire de nouveau aux douceurs de la vie.

FREEDOM

My dream is reality
We are free!
No more hiding
No more lying
No more false papers,
Nothing to trouble me.

I do not want to think about tomorrow.
For today we are all together
And here no one will harm us.

Is it true that I am free?
I think that I am drunk!
I let myself feel this delight
Because ended is the torture
Of always pretending
Without ever showing my true feelings.

But now all this is behind me.
And I yearn again for the sweetness of life.

Switzerland, May 23, 1944
Translated from the French

Switzerland

CLAPARÈDE

After crossing the border, we walked to Claparède, the transit camp in Geneva run by the Swiss Army. People were not supposed to stay there for more than a couple of days. They took identity photos, asked for our nationalities and dates of birth. At one point, they asked if any of us were Polish.

I had always been an Austrian citizen, but I liked Jacques Majerholc and he was Polish. Since I was afraid the Swiss would separate us, I stood with the Poles and that's the nationality that appears on my Swiss identity card.

The Swiss then asked me if I would stay in Claparède to work. That put me into a real quandary. After the thrill of being reunited with my peers, should I now be separated from them? At the same time I was very grateful for the safety the Swiss provided, so I said yes and stayed while the others left for the quarantine camp in Geneva called *Le Bout du Monde*—The End of the World.

At last I could begin keeping a journal, something I always wanted to do. Claparède was a busy place with refugees streaming in daily. I did laundry, dishes and whatever I was asked to do. My diary indicates that I didn't complain about the work. But other incidents limited my stay to 12 days.

I was supposed to be in my room by 9 P.M. One night, I had lots of dishes to wash and laundry to fold, so I stayed in the kitchen to finish the job. I was reprimanded, but not too severely because I was working.

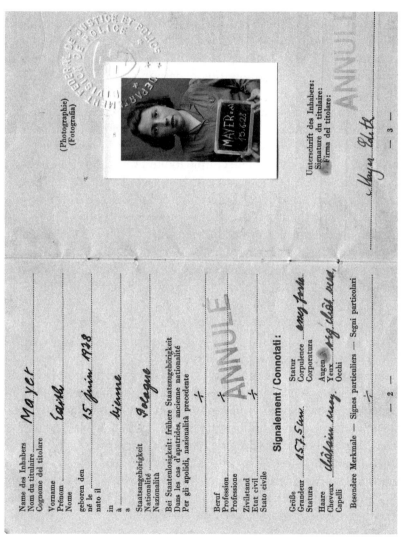

My Swiss identity card; wearing the blouse I made in Cahors.

The next day, Chameau (George Hamel), the oldest chieftain from the scout camp in Florac, arrived in Claparède. Somehow he managed to get into Switzerland. I was starved for news of the others and knew only too well what dangers they faced daily. We sat in the dining area to chat, so I went to bed late again and was reprimanded again, this time more severely.

I was angry about these reprimands because I worked hard, from morning until night, for no pay. I vented my frustration in my diary. I was not quite 16 and was never thanked. The Swiss afforded me little tolerance when I did nothing wrong except miss my exact bedtime.

The transit camp of Claparède was run by the Swiss army. With hindsight, I now think that they expected me to comply and obey like a soldier instead of acting like a cooperative, autonomous individual.

The last straw came when I saw a Jewish family being sent back into Nazi-occupied France. The couple looked Orthodox and had two teenage children, a boy and a girl. The Swiss would put the refugees in a van, drive them across the border and set them down in the middle of the road. I saw them put this family in the van. Since I knew what awaited them in France, I protested vigorously. This was too much for the Swiss. I was told that there had been complaints about me. I was promptly shipped off to the quarantine camp in a section of Geneva called Champel. I had spent less than two weeks in Claparède.

Excerpts from my diary/Translated from the French

Camp de Claparède, May 30, 1944

I am disgusted...I could pull out my hair. What is my mother doing? My father? Is he alive? My brother? What will become of me? What will become of us? Nothing but question marks. With whom to talk? Those who are here don't understand anything...When I see the barbed wire so close and on the other side people [are] going for a walk, free, free. Ah freedom, when will you be mine completely? I have it, but only partially. True, it's a lot, but [it's] not everything. It's been a long time, [I'm] always locked up, and this time behind barbed wire.

In the basement there is a room enclosed with barbed wire. It's called the prison.

Here is what triggered this mood. One of the leaders who had taken care of me in France arrived at the camp. He knows me and I was delighted to see him again. In the evening I talked with him because I knew that I would not be able to do so the next day. But I should have gone to bed at 9 P.M. and I did not go up to my room until 9:30.

You had to see how I got bawled out. It's useless to tell me that they want to keep me and then [they] treat me like a workhorse. To make things worse, they told me that, if that happened two or three times, I would be sent back to France because it is as if I had disobeyed an order, and an order is an order.

I should have asked for permission to stay downstairs longer if I wanted to chat. But the night before, when I was supposed to go to my room by 9 P.M., I finished the dishes instead and folded laundry, they chided me a bit, but nicely, and they seemed pleased to have everything done. So, to work like an idiot, what for? It's depressing. And then again this morning, another incident. It seems like nothing, but I have had enough...

Camp de Claparède, June 1st, 1944

I'm still here. Another incident. I am furious, I am boiling. You should have seen with what haughty tone I was spoken to. Fortunately I was not the only one to get bawled out. And then he says (it was a soldier): "If you want to stay here longer ..." as if I had been the one who asked to stay. "Once, twice, three times, okay. But now it's every day and several times a day. This morning the CO told me there were complaints about you, etc. etc."

This is really too much. And what promises they made to entice me to stay! Had I known it was going to be like this, I would not have stayed. I can't get over it. We are here to work and then we [get] treated like prisoners and worse. Every day there are criticisms and with a manner...you can just imagine. I have not calmed down yet, but I am laughing anyway, because I don't care about anything anymore.

SWITZERLAND
May 1944 to July 1945

I was sent to Champel after 12 days in Claparède. Normally, we were to remain in this quarantine camp for three weeks, however, there was an outbreak of scarlet fever (20 cases), diphtheria (four cases) and numerous cases of impetigo, so I ended up staying for three months. I spent my 16th birthday in that camp. This camp, too, was run by the Swiss Army.

There were about 117 people of various ages in the camp, from very young children to the elderly. We were housed in an old private residence with a large yard on an estate surrounded by barbed wire and guarded by armed soldiers. For washing, there were two troughs behind the building that had cold water trickling down through holes in a pipe.

By mutual agreement, women and men washed during different set hours. I would strip down to my underwear, but never beyond that. Fortunately, it was summertime, so the situation was bearable. The younger children who did not wash themselves came down with impetigo. They were sent to the hospital and scrubbed until they were as red as boiled lobsters.

I slept in a room with six other girls. Boards two inches thick by 10 inches high were nailed into the floor to make walls to hold the straw we slept on. Each of us was given a blanket and at night we were lined up side by side to sleep on the straw, with little space left to navigate around the room. Since we had only the clothes on our backs, the lack of space did not present any problem. I don't remember any of us complaining about that.

As the weeks wore on, the ambulance would come—sometimes more than once a day—to take people to the hospital. To control disease, the camp authorities took drastic measures: They burned all the straw we used as beds and distributed a fresh supply. They asked us to stay outside until 4 P.M., and before we were allowed back into the building they took everyone's temperature. Those with fever were shipped off to the hospital.

Toward the end of my stay there, I developed a painful sore throat and began running a fever. It felt like diphtheria all over again, but I knew that you could not get it twice. I was shipped off to the infirmary in an adjacent building called Le Val Fleuri. I spent a week recovering there and then was sent off to the Centre Henri Dunant, run by the International Red Cross.

When I left Claparède to rejoin the others in the camp in Champel, I was glad to be back with my peers. But life with teenagers with nothing to do and no adult presence is not all sugar and spice. One interesting phenomenon was that there were two groups of young people: those with whom I had crossed the border and the Zoot Suits and the Mods, with whom we didn't socialize.

My group always got together on Saturday nights to have an *oneg*, to sing and talk and dream about what we would do when the war was over. These *onegs* recaptured the flavor of our Friday nights in Florac. We were very idealistic, calling ourselves "the Maccabees," and we were going to work for a better world once the war was over.

In the other group the girls dressed provocatively and the boys had zoot suit hairstyles (hence the name we called them) that were very trendy. For entertainment, they held dances in their dorm room with one fellow bellowing out swing melodies using a megaphone. None of the adults had anything to do with either group and no one took an interest in us. We were left to our own devices.

On Fridays, a Jewish organization provided us with brown paper bags that contained *Shabbat* treats, usually an apple or an orange, a small pack of raisins, canned cream of chestnuts or a can of sardines. We would save most of it for our *oneg* on Saturday night. This showed much self-restraint on our part because when we got up from the dinner table we were often still hungry.

Books were not available. Once, someone got their hands on a copy of *Cyrano de Bergerac* by Edmond Rostand. We lined up to read it. There must have been 15 people ahead of me, and when my turn came I could not put the book down. I missed lunch because I kept reading. Such was the intellectual drought that confronted us.

A few people in the camp managed to obtain cigarettes, and some of my peers encouraged me to try. Felix from Vienna offered me a cigarette that I smoked without inhaling. He pointed out that I was not really smoking, so I inhaled and had a big coughing fit. That did it. Recollecting that Papa had gotten so sick from the nicotine, I concluded that smoking just wasn't worth it. I never smoked again.

I continued to keep my diary, where I put down my crushes and disappointments—all very adolescent stuff. There was one encounter with the Swiss, however, that I wrote down verbatim.

One day it happened that I spoke to a soldier guarding us. He told me about his family problems and then revealed that soldiers were forbidden to speak to us. *Le Bout du Monde* means "the end of the world," and that camp certainly felt like it.

Excerpt from my diary

July 6th, 1944

Now to the other adventure, still in Room 9. During the day our dear Henri installed a fine lighting system to allow us to stay up after "lights out." He had a light bulb [we could hide] in a closet during the day, then take out after the lights were turned off. This allowed us to spread our blankets out on what was left of our straw. This installation would have been superfluous if the gentlemen of Room 15 did not always stay in our room until 10 P.M., when they were kicked out unceremoniously by some camp official.

That night we were supposed to inaugurate this fine installation, so we did not rush to prepare our "beds" on our yellow "mattresses." We wanted to have something interesting to do in the blue light. I forgot to mention that the blue light bulb had been taken from the toilet. In addition to that, we had broken the light bulb in our room, so we had to replace it as well. We found another light bulb, so here we are with one broken [bulb] and two replacements. I should add that the toilets had no lights, except for moonlight. To add insult to injury, our friend [told] us to ask Pierre for another light bulb since we broke ours. In the end, he went and asked for one.

So here we are. [After] lights out we took our little blue bulb from the closet, we unscrewed the bulb from the ceiling, and everyone was delighted with the ingeniousness of our friend.

An unannounced visit from the head of the camp is a common occurrence, and this time was no exception. All of a sudden someone tried to open the door. I pushed long enough to allow someone to flip the switch and put out the light, and then I opened it. It was the head of the camp with Pierre.

"Since you know how to break light bulbs and how to replace them by swiping the ones from the hall or the toilets, you will have no light bulb until further notice. By the way, Pierre, take their bulb right away."

Upon hearing this, Henri climbed on the bench to unscrew the light bulb. But the head of the camp flipped the switch and our famous blue installation was turned on. I was scared. I was still standing by the door badly shaken, with my legs threatening to collapse, but I managed to stand.

"Now, now" he said, "what is this? I see, one light bulb is not enough. Pierre, take this one as well. Who is the head of this room?"

"It's me," said Moineau (her scout name meaning sparrow).

"Well, you will spend four days in prison. That'll teach you for next time."

At that point I was so indignant that I said, "If she goes, I will go too."

"Good, you will go as well. In fact, the whole room will go."

To which I replied, "If we have to."

He immediately responded, "And you will be sent back (to France) together, if necessary." He then slammed the door and left.

(This is why I reproach the Swiss. Ours was a very minor prank. Nevertheless, the only thing the Swiss could think of was to threaten us with a return to France and certain death.)

Now all the kids reproached me and told me I should not have said anything because it made everything worse, that I did the same thing the other boys had done with the fellow they put in prison, that I was wrong, etc. etc.

I was so shaken I could barely stand, but it is useless to talk about my feelings. The next morning all the girls were quiet, anxiously awaiting what would happen next. When I went down to get a broom, as representative of our room, I was told that we were all stupid girls. At breakfast we got another official reprimand by the head of the camp. The end of the story was that Room 9 had to clean all the windows of the building. This job was started, but not completed.

(Translated from the French.)
***

Since I was very insecure I accepted the opinions others had of me. Upon reading this passage 50 years later, I saw a different girl: a spunky girl who stood up to the Swiss; not an easy feat. But when I re-read the passage more recently, I saw that by speaking up I saved Moineau from four days in prison. My indignation came from the recognition that Moineau, who was a little older than the rest of us and a very serious, responsible young girl, had not been involved either in the planning or the execution of our scheme. I felt it was unfair that she should be the one to be punished. That's why I spoke up.

After I recovered from what must have been strep throat, a large group of children and I walked to Le Centre Henri Dunant, named after the founder of the Red Cross in Switzerland. It was housed in the former Hotel Carlton, an elegant edifice across the street from the Palace of the League of Nations.

We carried our little bags and walked through Geneva for over an hour. I was very aware of the fact that we looked like refugees and felt as though the word Jew was plastered on my forehead. I was tired of being a refugee and so much wanted to be just an ordinary kid.

When we got there, we were told to leave all our belongings in the front hall and were ushered into bathrooms where we were told to leave our clothes. Everything had to be cleaned and disinfected. Then we were washed. I objected strenuously since I was old enough to wash myself, but the woman in charge insisted. It was humiliating. Then, wrapped in towels, we were sent to the next room to be deloused. I already had short hair, but the other girls with long hair were given short haircuts and the boys had their heads shaved.

Then we were given some clothes from the *Schweizerische Kinderhilfe* and another week of quarantine followed. At least there were books to read and we slept in real beds—all welcome changes. At some point we were examined by a physician. I was diagnosed with tuberculosis, though my case was milder than some. I spent two weeks at the center before being sent to Alpina to recover.

I met Dolly Citroen at the center. She was a university student, young, very pretty, charming and dynamic. I kept in contact with her for quite a while. But the center was a transit place where we were being processed and soon we parted.

In August I was sent to Alpina in Chésières-Villars to recover.

I still remember my arrival in Alpina, above Bex-les-Bains, a small town beyond Montreux. I don't remember how we got to Bex to take the cable tram up the mountain, but I do remember the ride up

Alpina in Chésières-Villars.

the precipitous slope and how the tram hung over the abyss. When we got to the mountain top, which, though summer, still had visible snow-capped peaks, we walked to the sanatorium, a very modern building. Alpina was a privately-owned facility for children with tuberculosis. The owner, Mme. Rapa, made the home available to the Red Cross during the war because she had no clientele.

The sanatorium was built on the slopes, with all the windows facing south. It had six stories and each floor was recessed to allow the full sun to reach into the rooms on the floor below. There was a terrace on each floor, large enough to put out small beds for the children. The top floor had a game room with a ping-pong table. Out front, there was a playground with swings and a see-saw. (I had never seen one before and wondered what it was.)

A fellow by the name of Jacques Hepner, who later became a close friend, was leaning out the window looking down at us. He had a white compress around his neck, and that impressed me. I also met Leon Wodowski, called Leon Wodo by all, who would go on to become a lifelong friend.

I spent three months there. The first six weeks were lovely. There were many Jewish refugee children, all in the same boat with me. For a while Dolly Citroen worked there. While all was not sweetness and light—one counselor would punch us in the back at mealtimes to make us sit up straight—it was a welcome relief from what had gone on before.

Hot water for bathing was available only once a week, but I was so eager to wash that I took a cold shower every morning. The food was adequate and I even learned to play ping-pong.

During the previous year, in hiding and in Switzerland, I became religiously observant, falling back on the beliefs and practices of my early childhood. As a result, I refused to eat non-kosher meat. When the other children had meat meals, I was given a little triangle of processed Gruyere. After months and years of starvation, I should have eaten the meat but no one told me that, religiously, I was allowed to do so for the sake of my health.

Alpina had no books. So when Dolly left for Geneva, she arranged to send regular packages of books to Leon, Jacques and myself, who were considered the three musketeers. We would take turns reading them, and then sent them back so we could get new shipments.

All our bedrooms faced the Massif du Mont Blanc. Every morning I watched the sun rise and color the snow a tender pink. The majesty and grandeur of those mountains was awe inspiring. It was hard to imagine the madness and violence of the war raging so close by when

In Alpina.

I looked at the peace and beauty of Mont Blanc. That view saved my sanity.

On *Erev Rosh Hashanah* 1944, the staff prepared a nice dinner for us. I was getting ready to go to the dining room when I was handed a letter from the Red Cross. When I first came to Switzerland, I had given them whatever information I had about Papa and Kurt. This letter informed me that both were sent to the notorious transit camp, Drancy, outside of Paris and, from there, to Auschwitz. At the time, I had no idea what Auschwitz meant. While I frequently expressed my concerns about the fate of my family in my diary and prayed for them every night, not once did it occur to me that human beings were capable of doing what the Germans were doing to their fellow human beings. It would be many months before I found out.

We were given chores to do, like setting and clearing the tables. Leon volunteered for kitchen duty in order to get enough to eat: He scraped out the pots to get more food. Later, I helped out in the laundry. The laundress, Mme. Dufresne, was a Swiss peasant woman in her 30s who had no teeth. She often pointed to a cover girl on some magazine and told us that once upon a time she had teeth like that. Leon and I would look at each other and smile, but she was a very kind woman. When I worked with her in the laundry, she would not allow me to do some of the heavier work.

Before I left Chésières-Villars, I went to her house to say goodbye. She lived in a modest chalet with her husband and two children. She treated me to a big omelet and gave me a man's handkerchief and said, *"C'est un beau mouchoir"* ("It's a beautiful handkerchief"). This was a generous gift from her, since I knew she used rags for herself. (I still have that handkerchief.) This special woman taught me a huge lesson: Kindness and compassion have nothing to do with education, wealth or status in life. It can often be found among the humble. This woman was humble in a most unselfconscious way.

In late September all the Jewish children left. I realize now that they were sent to schools. I was not. They were replaced by teenage boys from rural areas in the Alsace-Lorraine region where heavy fighting was expected. These boys were different from the Jewish boys—they were rougher and vulgar, and I had nothing in common with them.

By then I was working in the laundry full-time. I also straightened out Mme. Rapa's room and washed her silk stockings every day. I stayed in Chésières until November. No one ever mentioned school to me and I did not know enough to ask about it.

Those last six weeks there were difficult. I had some run-ins with the nurse, there were no books—only detective stories—and my friends were gone. I was no longer happy to be there.

In November, in keeping with my request to be sent to *un home rituel*, a religious home, I was sent to work as a nanny in Ulisbach, near Winterthur, in the German-speaking part of Switzerland. Miriam and Henri Dybnis, called Dyb by his wife, were running a Jewish home for dozens of refugee boys between the ages of 8 and 14. My job was to care for their little baby, Monique.

The house they lived in was very cramped. The downstairs common room, called *die Stube*, was the only heated room in the house. It usually took me one hour to warm up enough to fall asleep at night. In the morning, my bedroom window was covered with frost on the inside, and snow blew in through the cracks. The room was equipped with a large pitcher of water and a wash basin, and I often had to break the ice in the pitcher before pouring water into the basin, that's how cold the room was. Once out of bed, I was cold for the rest of the day.

For months there was no one my age to talk to, and I missed that terribly. One entry in my diary reads: "If I don't get to be with kids my age soon, I think I'll go nuts."

After about three months all the children and I moved to Speicher near Trogen, about four kilometers west of St. Gallen in the Appenzell. The home was on a hilltop with a 360-degree view of the surroundings. From there you could look down on Lake Constance (Bodensee) and Germany to the north, the Austrian Alps to the east, the Saentis Mountain range to the south and St. Gallen to the west. It was a magnificent spot, and the Swiss Army had an observation post nearby.

Our new facility was a big four-story building made of wood, a real fire trap. It once served as an orphanage for Swiss children, but the few Swiss children in it were moved to another orphanage and we got the run of the place. I assume the authorities must have made a deal with Henry Dybnis to educate the boys because he arranged to have all the children schooled in-house. He called it Kinderheim Futura in Speicher.

The staff consisted exclusively of Jewish refugees with the exception of the nurse, who was Swiss. They were professional people who were competent teachers. On Fridays, classes would stop at noon, leaving time for the children themselves to clean the building for *Shabbat*. We had trouble getting a decent cook until they found an Austrian refugee who once owned a restaurant in Vienna. He cooked very well but because ritual slaughter was forbidden in Switzerland, everything we ate was dairy.

Monique and I, July 1945.

Kinderheim Futura in Speicher. Miriam, back row on the right, is yelling at one of the boys.

We got our milk from the farmer next door. Our cook poured the milk into large, shallow pans overnight, then skimmed off the fat to make butter...and so, we drank partially skimmed milk. I ate a lot and always went back for seconds. Sometimes I would even go to the kitchen between meals to get a snack. I was always hungry; perhaps I was making up for all the meals I had missed. I was getting plump, though I worked off most of the fat.

I was on my feet all day, six days a week with only Saturdays off, rising with Monique, feeding her three times a day, taking her out for walks. During her naps, I washed her diapers by hand, rinsing them in cold water and hanging them up to dry, outdoors or indoors, depending on the season. Every evening I gave her a bath and put her to bed. Miriam was too busy to care for her own daughter.

When I was done doing all that work, Miriam would order me to scrub the wooden floor in her apartment by putting steel wool under my feet and shuffling around the room, over and over again. She also had me clean the hair out of her hairbrush. At one point I developed severe cramps in the calves of my legs. The doctor who examined me said that it was because of my shoes; I wore inexpensive tennis shoes that provided no support. So Miriam bought me some old lady shoes. I was never paid, nor given any pocket money. I accepted all that. What was hard to take was Miriam's constant censure. She never left me alone. No matter what I did, she would continually criticize my efforts.

These shoes and the dress I was given for my trip back to France would be the only new items of clothing I received during my entire 14 months in Switzerland. The rest of the time I wore used clothing from the Swiss Aid to Children. None of this improved my self-esteem.

I had a lot of initiative. Once a little girl of about 9 or 10 came to the home after staying with a Swiss family for nine months. She told me they never washed her hair. So I washed her hair, and when I was done Miriam told me to wash her hair and I told her I already had. That, she approved of. But another little girl wanted a haircut, so I gave her one. Miriam yelled at me with such emotion, you would think that I had murdered the child. Yet I remember that I stupidly tried hard to please Miriam and looked to her for approval.

The biggest revelation came recently, when I reread a passage in my diary. After several months in the home I was notified that a family had been found for me. It meant Miriam would lose me, her nanny. It also meant she was very aware of the substandard way she treated me. Suddenly, she manipulated me by being nice and giving me little gifts. In my diary I wrote: "She is so nice, how can I leave?" I was blind and naïve. As soon as I turned down the offer, she reverted to her abuse.

My religious observance had sustained me during very difficult times, so you can imagine my despair when, during a Saturday morning service in this traditional environment, I began doubting God and lost my faith. It hit me so hard, I cried. After the service, when Miriam asked me why I was crying, I told her, and she dismissed my deeply existential crisis with a wave of her hand.

In the meantime, I lost another year of schooling and was desperate to get an education. I saw myself as young and healthy and thought that, after the war, I would need to work to help support my parents, who might be sick, especially my father. I still had no idea what Auschwitz meant, so I still hoped to see him and Kurt again.

I pleaded with Miriam to let me learn how to type and take shorthand. I also wanted to learn English. Jacquot, a 16-year-old boy in the home, was not working and was being tutored in math by one of the counselors, Mr. Fuchs. My roommate, Charlotte, who was my age and whose parents were friends of the Dybnises, was sent to school, but Miriam showed no interest in my welfare or my future. She wanted me as her personal servant and, when I escaped her clutches after the war, she tried to lure me back.

When I insisted on learning how to type, she gave me a book about typing, pointed to a typewriter in the office and said, "Go type." That's what I did, but not until the end of every day, after working my usual 10- to 12-hour day and putting Monique to bed. Miriam also gave me an old shorthand book, and I taught myself as much as I could.

After six months of pleading with her for English lessons, Miriam finally assigned Mr. Mandel to teach me English. He gave me a copy of *Englisch lernen ein Vergnügen (The Joy of Learning English)*, a textbook for adults. I met with him for 20 minutes, three times a week. He would check my homework, listen to my memorization and assign the next lesson. Six nights a week, from 8 to 10 P.M., I studied. That gave me 12 study hours for each contact hour. In three months, I finished the book. I knew my irregular verbs, had mastered basic grammar and absorbed a basic vocabulary. This came in handy when I finally resumed my formal education.

Mr. Mandel gave me André Gide's novel, *La Porte Etroite (The Narrow Gate)* to read. It was the story of a young man and a young woman from the same upper-crust milieu. They liked each other and were destined to marry. But she had religious aspirations and the wedding never took place. I was less than enthralled by the story, and shared my opinion with Mr. Mandel. He dismissed my reaction to the point of making me feel stupid, and didn't give me any more books to read.

In April 1945, several of us went to the movies to see a comedy with Laurel and Hardy. It was the only time I went to the movies during my entire stay in Switzerland. The program began with a newsreel, which is how most people got to see what was going on around the world. Everywhere in the world, newsreels were shown in movie theaters before the feature film was run. This newsreel showed the Allies marching into Germany and discovering the death camps. They showed the concentration camps, complete with gas chambers and crematoria. They showed the Gestapo's instruments of torture.

I was completely devastated. It was my first exposure to what the Germans had done. I was sobbing so loudly, they removed me from the theater. Without access to radio and newspapers, I wasn't able to learn more about what happened to my family and the rest of the Jews until I returned to France.

On May 8, 1945, Germany signed its unconditional surrender. The war, the nightmare, was over. It was time to count the dead. Every day at the home, news arrived to tell the children that their relatives were dead, murdered by the Germans and their collaborators. Some of the young boys sitting in their dorm rooms stared at the pictures of their beloved parents and cried. My heart went out to them. What could I say? I hadn't yet put the pieces together and still hoped that Papa and Kurt had survived.

There was an active search to find relatives anywhere in the world who would take in these sad Holocaust orphans. Children without relatives ended up in "orphanages" often run by the OSE (Oeuvre de Secours aux Enfants), the same organization that saved children during the German occupation. These places were not called orphanages but *Maisons d'Enfants* (Homes for Children).

As for me, after watching those newsreels, I wasn't sure if any member of my family, including Mama, had survived. I certainly was not going back to Austria. In France, I didn't have anyone and so I thought that, if no one survived, I would go to what was then Palestine. What else was I to do? I was an older teenager with no marketable skills.

But Mama had indeed survived. She was in Toulouse and knew where I was because someone had scribbled in the margin of my last letter to her, "Edith is in Switzerland." The Red Cross and the OSE tracked me down and, in July 1945, I returned to France and Mama.

Before I left, Miriam bought me a summer dress to go with my old lady shoes. She gave me 20 Swiss Francs and pushed me to buy a useless bracelet. More than 50 years later, when she was happily living in the U.S., I wrote her an honest letter that let her know exactly how much psychological damage I had to overcome because of her unconscionable attitude toward me.

On my way to France, I stopped in Zurich to see Otto Steinmetz, Putzi's younger brother. He was a year older than I and I discovered that he had become a Communist while serving time in a Swiss work camp. I stopped in Geneva and took one last swim in Lake Geneva at seven in the morning. Then, it was off to Toulouse.

During most of my time in Switzerland, I was utterly miserable. It was a fallow period of my life academically, except that I learned basic English and how to type. The sole benefit was that I was now healthy and strong, able to face the physical challenge of the hard years that lay ahead. But, and there is a large BUT, after I saw the newsreels and realized what had happened to my people, to Papa and Kurt and all of my murdered relatives, I fully appreciated how fortunate I was to have been spared the camp experience, and how incredible it was that I was still alive and functioning.

INTRODUCTION TO THE POST-WAR YEARS

The war years and post-war years were so filled that there is much to tell. Most people think that when the shooting stops it's all over and everyone can go back to the status quo ante. But when lives are so disrupted, you start from minus zero and it takes a very long time to pick up the pieces and put a life back together. That's one aspect of the Holocaust (or of any other similar situation) that is not usually talked about. And yet it is what we do with our freedom and, ultimately, with our opportunity that matters most, for during the crisis we have few choices.

France

TOULOUSE
1945-1946: A Year of Floundering

Denise, the *resistant* formerly known as Toubib, met me at the railroad station in Toulouse on a hot day in July 1945. I was glad to see her again. She had often taken me from one hiding place to another, and was with us in Florac. Today she was bringing me to the subsidized restaurant where Mama usually ate lunch. When we got there, Mama was overjoyed to see me. The feeling was mutual.

After lunch, I took my little suitcase in hand and we took the streetcar to the last stop. We then walked a good half hour to her place on the Chemin des Sept Deniers. She'd rented a small room with kitchen privileges from an older woman, a masseuse by profession. Mama slept on the bed and I slept on a box spring. My mattress was covered with wool, so I removed it because summers in Toulouse could be very hot.

I did not know if Mama was aware of Papa's and Kurt's deportations from Drancy to Auschwitz. For many weeks we tip-toed around the subject of Papa's and Kurt's fate, trying to gently break the news to each other. It was almost a relief when we discovered we both knew the awful truth. Though we still hoped they had both survived, the bitter reality of their murders gradually sank in.

Because of our long separation, we had to become used to each other again. With me no longer a child, Mama tried her best to be nice, albeit with less and less success. There were issues that needed to be addressed—my education, the matter of housing and of making ends meet, as well as the unspoken issue of how to deal with the recent traumas. And so, from July 1945 to August 1946, we were in transition, with frequent changes and searches for answers on many fronts.

Adjusting to living in a big city did not come easily to me. I was disoriented because I was used to being led around by counselors. As a result, I frequently got lost and would sometimes take the streetcar in the wrong direction. And though I disliked group living, it took me a while to get used to being on my own.

In addition, I would go stir crazy in the tiny room I shared with Mama. I was used to working from morning until night, but now in Toulouse there was nothing for me to do. I often sang all the songs I learned to get rid of my excess energy. There were some girls in the neighborhood with whom I could have become friendly, but I didn't socialize with them because we had little in common.

When the war ended, the horrors of the Holocaust were made public and displayed for the first time. (The persecution and mass murder of the Jews hadn't yet been named the Holocaust. The so-called Final Solution was called "atrocities of the war against the Jews.") There were exhibits, publications with photographs and books. The press was full of what the Germans and their collaborators had done.

I went to the exhibits and looked at the pictures with horror and disbelief. I had to know, yet the facts devastated me. My whole world crumbled. It seemed the good people were murdered while the evil ones survived. Life seemed meaningless, unfair, unjust and not worth living. I contemplated suicide after having gone through so much trouble to stay alive.

I had to decide. If I chose to live, what kind of life would I create for myself? Should I take a straight and narrow path, like a nun, and cut myself off from the world? I was used to poverty and was chaste, but I could not take a vow of obedience. What if I made a selfish life for myself, doing whatever I wanted to do without regard for others? Those who did so seemed to prosper—Nazis who got away, collaborators and traitors. No, I couldn't do that either.

Why bother to strive for a better life? Why not indulge solely in pleasure? What was the point of being ethical? Effort to lead a just and ethical life, as far as I was concerned, seemed to be a waste of time. The daughter of one of the survivors, a tall, attractive young woman, became the mistress of a wealthy Frenchman, much older than she. She would stop at the café where her parents traded in the black market, in her expensive fur coats, often accompanied by her lover. Was she right?

In Switzerland I had lost my faith in God on that *Shabbat* morning and was dismissed by Miriam as if I were a fool. After Auschwitz, how could anyone contemplate the possibility of a benevolent, merciful God? The bearded Jews with their pious manner and black market activities were nothing but hypocrites to me. I was confused, my values and beliefs foundering on the rocks of the war. I turned my back on traditional Judaism, but I still had a strong sense of right and wrong.

To make matters worse, the mood among the French was no better. Hatred flourished along with cries for justice and revenge. But we all knew that justice could not rectify the abominations the Germans and their collaborators had committed. I could not understand how a human being could be nice to his own child and then brutalize another child in front of its mother.

Some Jewish children my age thought only of having fun and catching up on lost time (*ils ne pensent qu'á s'amuser*), but I could not. I needed existential answers. My quest was intense—to the exclusion of other, more mundane things. Answers came slowly. It took years, and I did not find them in Western religions or Western thought. I did not discuss these struggles with Mama, though I did express them in my diary.

In Toulouse, I joined the MJS, Mouvement de Jeunesse Sioniste, went to meetings and participated in long discussions. While my peers all had more education than I did, there was nothing wrong with my ears, so I listened and learned.

I had no understanding of political events and objected to girls serving in the Haganah, the army, in what was then Palestine. At one meeting, one of the young men said that they used young people to fight because older people refused to be cannon fodder—or words to that effect. That turned me off, though I remained a Zionist.

Mama was not thrilled with my attendance at these meetings. Her goal was to get us to America. Immediately after the war, she signed us up for the American quota. There was a five-year wait for applicants born in Austria, but I was not about to sit idle and twiddle my thumbs while waiting for my number to come up. I began to build a life in France.

In the post-war years, about one-third of the French people voted for the Communist party. After the war, there was a clear political battle for minds and votes. The Communist Party rented a large storefront in the heart of town, opposite the United States Information Agency (USIA). While the Communist store's windows were full of propaganda—with books, flags and slogans—the USIA displayed posters showing life in

America. There were houses for workers and photos of private houses with front yards enclosed by white picket fences. It looked too good to be true for, in my experience, only rich people lived like that. In my ignorance, I did not know what to believe.

The Communist slogans sounded so idealistic: "From each according to his ability, to each according to his needs." Of course, I did not know the truth, but I had a gut feeling that all was not as rosy as the Communists would have us believe. I withheld judgment. This was fortunate for, had I joined the party, I would not have been admitted to the United States.

Politics and philosophies of life aside, it was clear we needed to get out of the tiny room we were in, but housing was in very short supply. Then Mama learned through an acquaintance that a tiny apartment was available on the rue des Princes. The rent was affordable, just 500 French francs a month. But the tenants, a Jewish couple, wanted three times the rent for key money. Somehow Mama came up with 1,500 francs. For some reason, our new landlady continued to charge us pre-war rates. Sometimes I spent more on my weekly public showers than we spent on rent, but even so it was often difficult to come up with those 500 francs every month.

The house was on a narrow and hilly street. The nearest streetcar stop was down the hill, about 10 minutes away. I walked to town and school most of the time, since carfare was beyond our means. The house was built of stones and mud that was visible where the plaster was peeling. The exterior was cracked with broken stucco. After a rain I could see dampness creeping up the walls.

The neighborhood was mixed and safe, with some older houses and blue-collar families mixed in with gleaming new villas. The house had four apartments. One neighbor, Mme. Rigal, worked as a cleaning lady now and then and her husband worked in a factory. An old, unwashed couple lived across the hall. The husband worked in a shoe factory.

The apartment had one small room and a tiny kitchen with a tiled floor. There was no running water—the fountain, the source of our water, was half a block away. Each day I filled a pail and large pitcher several times and carried them back to the apartment. Every night I made sure the pitcher and bucket were full so there would be enough water to wash in the morning. The kitchen sink allowed water to drain into an open gutter. I washed clothes in the kitchen and then went out to the fountain to rinse them. While this was not too difficult in the summer, it was rough in the winter because the water was so cold.

The house I lived in from 1946 to 1952.
There were four two-room apartments. (Photo taken in 1956.)

The fountain at the end of the block where I went for water and to rinse my laundry. (On a later visit in 1956 with my friend Huguette.)

The apartment was cold in the winter because even though there was a small wood-burning stove in the kitchen, often we couldn't afford to buy the wood needed for heating—though we did have an old gas cook-top provided by the gas company.

There were no conventional toilets. In the rear courtyard there was an outhouse, Turkish style, with a cement floor and a hole in the middle. Shared by the four tenants, it was emptied about once every nine months, when a sanitation truck would come by and pump out its contents. Unfortunately, the neighbors often "missed" the hole, and I got so disgusted that I cleaned the place every week with an old broom and carbolic acid diluted in water. I hoped the neighbors would get the hint and help by taking their own turns cleaning the latrine. Mme. Rigal did it a few times, but the others did not, so Mama forbade me to continue cleaning it. (Before I came to America I thought I was constipated. But once I got to the "land of the free," I realized it wasn't me, it was the lack of decent toilets that caused my "condition.")

A curtain separated our main room from the kitchen. Mama slept on the bed in the big room that also held a large table that she used for work, three chairs and a small unpainted chest she got from a charitable organization. She bought a used armoire from the previous tenant and, later, we were given a foot-operated sewing machine by ORT.

I slept on a folding bed in the kitchen. The Rigals lent us a folding table, so during the day I folded the bed and pushed it against the wall. Then I would unfold the table, where we ate our meals and I did all my homework. At night I folded the table, put my books on a chair and opened my bed. Next to the chair there was a small alcove with two shelves and a bar to hang clothes.

Mama still had no marketable skills. She ended up working in sweatshops in the burgeoning garment industry. At first she worked for a furrier, sewing on buttons and linings, then as a presser. She was frequently fired because she was invariably late for work.

(After I earned my *Baccalauréat* in 1949, I worked intermittently, as jobs and my school schedule permitted. By the time I got to the university, we lived on my scholarship money and Mama no longer went to work.)

Through it all, I maintained contacts with the OSE. Martha, a member of the *Sixième* during the war, filled me in on the fate of some of my saviors: Her brother Souris had been killed, as had Giraffe, who had been captured and shot by the Germans. She had bravely carried on.

The OSE tried to help me. After my experiences in Switzerland, I wanted to be a professional working with young children. All the arrangements were made for my training in a different town, but Mama decided she would not let me pursue this goal. After our separation during the war, she was not about to lose me again.

I was interviewed by an OSE vocational guidance counselor who spent an hour and a half with me after Mama prevented me from getting the training I wanted. She concluded that I needed a *Baccalauréat*, something I was already aware of. The OSE couldn't help me anymore, so I had to find other avenues to get to where I wanted to be.

I tried correspondence courses that Mama helped pay for, but they were too difficult. Having had little formal schooling, I needed systematic coaching under the direction of a teacher, for I knew nothing. But at 17, I was too old to go back to the *lycée* and start from scratch.

When Mama learned that I knew basic English, she wanted me to further advance my studies and paid for private English lessons. The teacher, a nice woman, did not give me a grammar or a workbook. She asked me to read and translate a novel, but I didn't have enough vocabulary to do it well. The English lessons turned out to be a waste of time and money, but the teacher became a friend who listened as I unloaded my woes in French—especially about the continuing deterioration of my relationship with Mama.

Then I enrolled in Cours Pigier, a private business school. I asked to continue studying the old shorthand method I taught myself in Switzerland, and they said that was fine. I was also able to practice my typing. I went to classes in the mornings and had a part-time office job in the afternoons.

In the meantime, I told everyone I knew that I wanted to go back to school. As luck would have it, I met two women in the local subsidized restaurant, Frau Freund and her daughter, who were social workers. They suggested that I contact a Mme. Ginodman, a social worker in Moissac who had limited funds available for scholarships. An appointment was arranged and I met Mme. Ginodman in Moissac. She gave me a single year to do six years' worth of work in the *lycée* and earn the first *Baccalauréat*. If I had realized what I was getting myself into, I might have asked for two years. But I was not given a choice. It was one school year or nothing. I accepted the challenge and was introduced to Mlle. Denise Noyon, who ran a private school in Toulouse.

Mama and Mme. Ginodman accompanied me on my first interview with Mlle. Noyon, a petite, middle-aged woman with an assertive manner. We were led into a comfortable, dark living room where she and I argued over German grammar. She insisted that I learn it and I said I could not. Now I can teach German grammar, even without a textbook, but then it seemed to be an insurmountable difficulty. The argument ended in a draw.

Later, she told me that this was her way of testing me. She took me on a trial basis for one month and made no promises of success given the amount of catching up I had to do. School started on October 1, and I started private classes with her on September 1. I was happy and excited. Mlle. Noyon helped me get back on my feet, and exerted a powerful influence on me.

Soon after I came to Toulouse, I met Françoise in the subsidized restaurant. She was to become a dear friend. Six months older, taller, well-dressed, slender, with shoulder-length curly black hair, dark eyes, regular features and a full, sensuous mouth, I thought she was strikingly beautiful. She lived with her father; her mother and little sister had been murdered during the war.

Françoise worked in a small film distribution agency, Filminter. She helped me get a part-time job there and, when the manager was absent, we would talk a lot and waste time. Once, during a heavy downpour, we made little paper boats and threw them from our second-story window into the gutter and watched them sail away.

The office building we worked in was on a street leading to the Lycée de Garçons (high school for boys). Lined with bookstores, boxes filled with second-hand books were put out on the sidewalk for passersby to browse through. I always partook of this intellectual feast. Because these books were incredibly cheap, I could finally afford to buy some. I picked up a number of classics that way. One book that left me puzzled was *Madame Bovary* by Gustave Flaubert. I could not understand that woman. She had a perfectly good husband and was throwing him away. She spent money well beyond her means and, above all, neglected her child. How could she do that? Living through the experiences I had just lived through, Emma Bovary was incomprehensible to me. It took years before I understood her character.

I was often late for work because it took an hour each way to get back and forth from the furnished room to the office, and the idea of packing a sandwich had not yet crossed the Atlantic. The subsidized restaurant closed after a while, and other eateries were prohibitively expensive, so I had to go home for lunch. An old, small injury to my calf gave me cramps when I walked fast and that did not help me get to the office on time, either.

One day, Françoise's father and Mama decided to send the two of us to the opera to see *Cosi fan Tutte* by Mozart. The show was dazzling, but Françoise and I couldn't figure out what was going on because we didn't know the story and there were no translations or surtitles available. Still, we had a marvelous time!

Françoise and I spent lots of time talking about the pain our parents inflicted upon us. Her father was a difficult man, and life with Mama was one of constant crises and emotional outbursts. On the rare occasions when we went out with members of the opposite sex, Françoise got all the attention. At 17 I still looked much younger, and was badly dressed in hand-me downs from various charities. Make-up or lipstick weren't part of my world either.

That summer Françoise and her father decided that she would go to Cheltenham, England, to live with her aunt. The objective was to spend a year there and learn English. We parted tearfully and promised to write.

Then, out of the clear blue sky, Miriam Dybnis sent me an invitation to come and visit her family. She and her husband were running a *Maison d'enfants* (home for children) in Malmaison, a suburb of Paris. She offered to let me stay with her for free. I jumped at the opportunity, and with Mama's blessings I left for Paris at the beginning of August 1946 to spend a month with them.

Monique did not remember me, so I had to curb my enthusiasm. She had grown up, and her mother had trained her in good table manners. The Dybnises also had a son who was being cared for by a nanny. On that trip, Miriam was very nice to me. She didn't criticize me and allowed me to spend my days as I wished. Little did I know that she had an ulterior motive.

I had a nice month. I visited Josephine de Beauharnais's castle in Malmaison; I went swimming in the Seine and came out covered with oil. It's a miracle I did not get sick! Leon was still in Switzerland, but I saw Otto Steinmetz and Jacques Hepner while I was there.

Both of Jacques's parents had survived the persecution as had his twin sister, and they reclaimed their apartment in Paris. Jacques looked well in a stylish suit, and wore modern, rimless glasses. Leon and I thought he was a very lucky boy, but we sensed that something was desperately wrong. Jacques committed suicide several years later.

Otto's story was different. He was 19 and working at *Paris-Match*, the well-known picture magazine. He was a dedicated Communist who spent his nights putting up Communist posters. This was against the law, and, if he was caught, could have landed him in jail. He also didn't bother continuing his education. That, I thought, was a mistake and I told him so, but he had eyes only for Marxist ideology.

We met under the Arc de Triomphe on the Champs Elysées. He told me that the concierge's daughter was running after him but that he was not interested in her. He talked to me about free love. I encouraged him to get more schooling and to work for his own future. We promised to write.

As August came to an end and I made my preparations to leave, Miriam asked me to stay and take care of her little boy. So that's why she had invited me to Paris! I was surprised just the same. Didn't she realize I was going back to school? I told her about it, but she didn't believe me and poo-poohed the idea. She told me it was an impossible task and not even worth a try. I left without her moral support. When I did pass the *Baccalauréat* at the end of that academic year, I happily wrote to her about my success. Her response was pure acid: "It's not passing the exams that counts, it's only what you absorb."

While I resumed my secular education, my sex education was non-existent because Mama had the most Victorian views. Sex was a dirty word. To be pregnant was embarrassing. When I asked her why, she said that it showed the whole world you had sex with your husband! To this I replied: "Of course you have sex with your husband."

I was almost 18 years old and felt it was time to get the true facts about the birds and the bees. I bought a book, *Au service de l'amour* (*In the Service of Love*) written by a doctor. It gave me anatomy, physiology and words of advice. While I did not agree with everything (for instance, he said it was okay to have intercourse during a woman's period), at least I felt informed. My curiosity was satisfied.

In general, though my views on morality were rigid, this was to get worse under the influence of my new teacher. It would be many years before I would mellow and strike a balance.

TOULOUSE II
1946-1947: School at Last

Starting with September 1946, I got very little sleep. In the French system, the *Baccalauréat* is a rigorous exam graded by teachers who don't know you. Grades earned during the year do not count, but the academic achievement reflected by those grades must be extensive. With all due respect to Miriam, you can't earn your *Baccalauréat* unless you have retained what you have learned.

It was a year of enormous effort and single-mindedness. I did nothing but study: no dates, no movies, no outside jobs, no sports except on Sunday mornings when I went for a walk or a swim. Fortunately, I was in good health and could handle the physical rigors. I got up every morning at 6 A.M., did my exercises, and walked to school where I spent the entire day, except for lunch hour. I studied at least until midnight—seven days a week.

Three people gave me moral support: Denise Noyon, my current teacher, Mme. Brun from Nice and Mlle. L., the English teacher from Mende. I corresponded with them regularly. Mama did not realize what I was up against, but was willing to give me a chance. Everyone else thought I was facing an impossible task and would fail.

I absorbed knowledge like a sponge. I was fluent in German, had some background in English and could read, write and spell French without mistakes. I knew my arithmetic and my multiplication tables. I could write a half page essay without difficulty. I had to learn how to write literary research papers. This required knowledge of French literature, the history of ideas and the ability to organize my thoughts and present them in a coherent fashion.

I had to learn algebra, geometry and solid geometry. I also had to improve my vocabulary and do more reading in English literature. In German I did not have to do much, but I was petrified that they would ask questions about German grammar. That's why I took English as my first language and German as my second language.

I started my studies bright and early on September 1. My first assignment was to write a self-portrait. Straightforward as usual, I had nothing good to say about myself: I thought I was unattractive, fat, stupid and ill-tempered (*mauvais caractère*). I also thought that I had a mental bloc for math. I only saw one positive aspect and that was that I had a lot of goodwill. While writing and thinking about myself I discovered that I also had courage. This insight came in handy for the rest of my life and helped me face many more challenges.

Mlle. Noyon started me on Latin, and loaded me up with reading assignments and algebra. She gave me seven pages of equations to complete in one night. I brought them back without a single mistake. While I showed an understanding of the material, she also noted that my accomplishment showed tremendous powers of concentration. When she asked one of the other students whether this meant she should give me more or less homework, he said less. She said no, I should get more. I never complained.

When the math went well, she dropped the Latin so I could concentrate on math and French literature and keep up with my English.

Then came a bombshell.

I had been throwing up once a month, like clockwork. Each time, Mama found a way to blame me: it was something I ate away from home, or I went out with my coat unbuttoned and caught a cold in my stomach. She was full of *bubbeh meises* (grandmother's tales).

In July, before I went to Paris to see Miriam, I had another episode. I did not want to see a doctor so I asked Mama to get me a laxative. I was so insistent that she went to the pharmacist and told him why. He told her he'd be glad to sell her one but, he said, if I had appendicitis, it could kill me. With that I had to yield and see a doctor.

Dr. Cohen came to the house. When I came back from Switzerland we had gone to see him because I wanted to lose some weight. He said that he would have to give me shots and check my heart frequently because there was some danger. Because I had just gone through some serious illnesses, I was not about to jeopardize my health. I said no. Though he was married, Françoise had once told me that he'd made a pass at her. I thought it was because she was so pretty. But then he tried the same thing with me. I never went back to him alone, though I did not tell my mother about him.

Dr. Cohen examined my belly and said I had chronic appendicitis. He said there was no urgency, but the appendix should come out. I went for the medical exam to a public hospital where the surgeon who examined me was surrounded by medical students, some of whom I knew. I was embarrassed to lie there with my belly exposed. I was told that I had a choice of whether or not I wanted my appendix taken out. A time was tentatively set for September.

With my academic workload I was not about to take time out to have an appendectomy, especially since the surgeon was iffy about it. Mama went to see Mlle. Noyon and asked her to prevail upon me to have it removed. She did so, and a go ahead decision was made. I had the surgery done as a public charity case. Before I went in, Mlle. Noyon gave me a pile of books to read while I recuperated.

The hospital was run by the Sisters of St. Vincent of Paul, who wore big, royal blue woolen skirts and large, white starched hats shaped like funnels. They led us in the "Our Father" prayer every morning and evening.

I was placed in a ward with 20 other patients. On the morning of the surgery, someone ordered me to walk down to the operating room in my hospital gown and to get there by 10 A.M. The surgeons were running late, so I had to wait, standing in the chilly fall air. Then a bloody accident victim was brought in, so I had to stand there and wait until noon. Finally, my turn came. They put me to sleep with ether, and the next thing I knew I was in my bed and an orderly was slapping my cheeks to wake me up.

By then it was 1 P.M. and visiting hours were commencing. As soon as Mama showed up, the orderly left and I threw up from the ether. I wanted to be a hero in front of my mother, but my nausea defeated me.

For two days I received neither food nor water. For seven days after that I was only allowed liquids. Moving my right leg was painful because they had cut into muscle tissue. Coughing or laughing was painful. After nine days they took out my stitches and sent me home. I'd lost 10 pounds.

I now no longer had a bloated abdomen; my stomach was flat. So that's what it was! The surgeon later told me that my appendix was very inflamed and it was a good thing that it had been removed.

After a few days at home, Mlle. Noyon pleaded with me to return to school: she was holding up her math lessons until I came back. Two weeks after surgery, I was back in school, I left my books at home and rode the street car instead of walking. During my medical absence, I read only some of the books she had given me.

By now Mlle. Noyon had a full complement of students, ranging in age from 12 to 18. We were an odd lot. There were two music majors there who were studying at the Conservatory for half a day. Because no public school could accommodate their schedules, the rest of their academic studies necessitated their tutelage by Mlle. Noyon. Then there was Anne Marie and her sister who came from a well-to-do family from Blagnac. Anne Marie was very bright and pretty, and her parents wanted to speed up her education. There were a couple of other students as well who needed the special attention a small school would provide.

In addition, there was a girl like me, who was preparing for her *Brevet Elémentaire*, an exam covering the first four years of *lycée*. She had two years to catch up. Mme. Ginodman had also sent two 19-year-old Jewish boys who told us they wanted to write poetry and were interested in learning. But they did not study, and were gone within a month.

And now the fun really began. The pressure was on; I was working full steam. I covered the first three years of *lycée* algebra without difficulty. Plane geometry was all right, but when algebra was combined with solid geometry, I slowed down.

I was learning new material every day and doing equations every night. But as things got more difficult I needed more time to work with the material. I had to keep moving forward and began having difficulties in solving problems. My mantra before going to sleep and before doing math was *"Mon esprit est lucide"* (My mind is clear). I always told myself I could do it.

If I told Mlle. Noyon that I stayed up until 1 A.M. to work on my problems, she'd say "Then stay up till 3 A.M." Of course, I always got up at six no matter when I went to bed. The neighbors complained that I woke them up when I pulled my bed over the tile floor, so I pulled it out earlier, but without opening it because then there would be no room for the table.

During the school year of 1946-47, rationing was still the rule. My diary on May 3, 1947 tells the story of a painful episode with Mama. Mama asked me to go to the bakery the day before and buy bread with rationing coupons that were about to expire. I forgot. This led to an incredibly angry explosion on her part. In my diary it was a matter-of-fact entry of several pages, in the style of Cyrano de Bergerac's *Gazette*. I'll let the diary tell the story:

"Latest news: this morning, at 8 A.M., my mother threw me out. It is with deep regret that I realize my mother is crazy. Sad, but true.

"She started by beating me while screaming abominably, with the laughter of a Fury and an animal satisfaction in her eyes. Her face was lit up and I saw a sadist in front of me in the process of satisfying her instincts. As I defended myself, pinching her to make her let go of my hair that she was pulling hard, she started to hit me even harder, pinching me, twisting my mouth, my nose and hitting my face.

"I remained silent, my face closed, eyes dry, looking at her as a spectator, but with a feeling of deep sadness because I realized that my mother was crazy, her passions unleashed. I was the only person on whom she could vent her animal instincts, and she took advantage of that.

"Then she started to cry, her face congested, eyes red and white saliva coming out of the corners of her mouth. It was horrible to see. I who love beauty, who want to see only beauty…Alas! My mother is crazy. What to do? We can't put her into an asylum?

"From time to time she would let go, with screams that would break the heart of a stone. I was not moved. I looked. I waited…for the end. Once she twisted the ring finger on my left hand which weakened my hand. Then she came back, twisting my face the way you twist laundry, beating me as if I were a carpet to get rid of its dust. I was a little handicapped because of my left hand, but I held onto her arms anyway. With her arms held and unable to do as she pleased, she found nothing better to do than to bite me. So be it. Finally, she sought to take away my keys, searching in my schoolbag, my pockets, in all my things, but unable to find them. In the process she took away some vitamins that were in my bag. Fortunately, they only cost four francs, so I'll be able to replace that. I feared that she would find the 70 francs I had economized on a thousand little things and that I will need now.

"Finally she allowed me to look for the keys by myself. But I didn't remember where they were. I heard her scream, swearing that I would not put a foot outside the door before handing her the keys. Maybe I was wrong. I don't know myself. But there was no other solution. And when I finally found the keys, I gave them to her without hesitation. I managed to stop her from shoving me when I left and I walked out with my usual greeting and a 'see you later.'

"At one point she had tried to drag me out of the apartment by pulling my sweater, and she tore it in the process. During the entire assault I remained calm. At the beginning, I was perfectly calm, although my hands were trembling. I think I was breathing faster. That's all. But I did not cry, did not feel like crying, I just looked. Once outside I could not hold back a few tears. It was the reaction. I walked slowly, arriving at the edge of the canal. I tried to get hold of myself. It was difficult. I was thinking of the previous night when my mother had come home at 10:30.

"I had started to study in bed; everyone was asleep. Then she started to talk to me. She spoke for at least a half an hour, in a monolog, sometimes raising her voice, always insulting me, swearing, promising me lots of unpleasant things, sometimes stopping to catch her breath, but only to start up again with more vigor. At first I tried to study in spite of her, but since she kept going, I closed my books and notebooks and crawled under the quilt, stuffing my ears. Since I could hear her anyway, I began to talk to myself, repeating always the same thing in a low voice, so as not to hear what she was saying: 'You bug me, you bug me, you bug me.' Then I got upset. I began to cry. Finally I prayed for help. When she had enough, she stopped and I, very calm, fell asleep. My only regret was that I had not studied."
(Translated from the French)

I went to school with my books. When I came back in the evening she was not home and the door was locked. I waited on the back porch until 10 P.M. I was locked out and did not know what to do as I had no idea where she was nor when she would be back. And I had not eaten.

There was a home for Jewish children in town so I went there and asked to spend the night. It wasn't too far from our house and I was sure they would take me in. But I could not study. The place was filled with noisy younger children and there was no room set aside for study.

The next morning I went back to school, unprepared for class. During the day my mother showed up, angry. She accused Mme. Ginodman and Mlle. Noyon of wanting to take away her child. My mother dragged me, the social worker and I think the teacher, to the police station. The *commissaire* (police captain) listened first to my mother's complaints. Then he questioned the social worker. When my turn came, he asked me what I wanted. I told him I wanted to be left alone to study. I don't know whether he expected me to be a juvenile delinquent but he looked puzzled and dismissed us with a wave of his hand.

My mother had frequent, high-decibel emotional outbursts wherein she criticized and blamed me for everything that wasn't right in the world. Initially, I shouted back, but Mlle. Noyon advised me to stop responding. When her shouting was too much for me, I left the apartment and waited at the entrance of the house for her rage to subside. Then I would go back in. She remained a constant source of pain and anguish during all the years we were forced to live together, and beyond.

During those years, I kept up my correspondence with my friends from Switzerland, including Leon, Jacques and Otto. My mother was in the habit of opening all my mail, even mail from my former teacher, Mme. Brun. When she discovered that Otto was talking to me about free love, she went ballistic and forbade me to correspond with him, as though anything could have happened between us with me in Toulouse and him in Paris.

No matter. I recalled that she had done the same thing to my brother in Genoa. Mail was very important for me. As a result of her tampering with my mail, I ended up getting a box in the post office and stopping there several times a week to see if there were letters for me. A letter from a friend could make my day, since in those days I had no close friends in Toulouse.

Françoise was gone for a year; eventually we drifted apart. When she came back from England, she commented on how much I had changed while she was the same, only more so. We parted as friends, since there is no reason people can't stay on good terms even if they change or drift apart.

During my year at the Cours Noyon my mother lost her job. My scholarship covered my tuition and gave me a tiny subsidy, so my mother found work with a furrier. She sewed linings into fur coats and put on buttons. This was piece work she could do at home. Every morning I carried two fur coats along with my books and dropped them off at the furrier on my way to school. I picked up two more coats after school. This went on for quite some time, until my mother found another job.

I thought my mother was old, probably typical of teenagers who think that way about people over 30. In 1945 my mother was only 42 years old. She was in her prime, but she acted like an old person. She walked slowly, had me do all the heavy work around the house, and had me carry her bags in addition to my book-filled schoolbag. She gained back all the weight she had lost during the lean war years and now weighed almost 200 pounds.

I tried to make up for what my mother had lost. Losing a husband and son in the Holocaust was unbearably painful. She focused on their

My mother after years of hunger, 1944.

My mother in one of her softer moments, Toulouse, 1952.

pain in the immediate postwar years and for the rest her life. If she woke up during the night, she would dwell on their anguish. When she ate something good, she had trouble enjoying it. She mourned her son more than she did her husband. Once I took her to see an operetta in Toulouse and she felt guilty for having a nice evening "when...." She surrounded herself with books on the Holocaust and tried to make me feel guilty by declaring that I did not remember Papa and Kurt.

I tried for a long time to make up for her losses until I realized that you cannot replace someone else–and it wasn't healthy to try. Over the years she compared me to my poor dead brother, insisting that HE would have been a better child...It is futile to compete against the dead. She was cruel and once blamed me for his death. What twisted thinking caused her to arrive at that conclusion is beyond me. Fortunately for my sanity, I rejected her views.

I made allowances for her behavior. I was raised on "Honor thy father and mother..." until one day the wisdom of the author of the Ten Commandments struck me: He did not say, "Thou shalt love thy father and mother...," only honor. That I could do. This realization removed the guilt I felt for not loving her. And yet love is what she craved more than anything else. On her deathbed her next-to-last words to me were: *"Du hast mich nie lieb gehabt"* ("You never loved me"). Of course, this was not so. The truth was that she destroyed that love.

On top of everything else, my mother was very bossy and treated me like a young child. During another doctor's visit, the physician told her I was growing up and she should give me more independence. When I heard that, I whispered *"Mir aus der Seele gesprochen"* ("My feelings precisely"). My mother got very angry and left in a huff. It must have been pretty obvious for him to notice it in the course of a brief visit.

She never shared her concerns with me and I was never part of her decision-making process. There were a couple of Jewish widows and a widower nearby and she spent her evenings and weekends talking to them. I never questioned this at the time, but now that I have grown children, I find this strange.

Confronting the horrors of the Holocaust, dealing with my mother, coming to terms with life as I saw it, all these things were all on my mind as I pursued the one thing that would liberate me, my education. These were tall orders for a teenager.

After the war, the bookstores were filled with new editions of Kafka, Heine and Brecht along with Maurois, Sartre, Camus and many others. Among the books on display in the store windows were many describing Eastern thought: Books on Hinduism and Buddhism sat side by side with existentialism.

Given the horrors we had just experienced, Judaism's basic tenets provided neither answers nor explanations—I only saw needless suffering. To this day, when I attend a religious service or a bar mitzvah, I can't help but ask myself, "For this they killed us?"

Christianity, through my limited knowledge of those beliefs, fared no better. Neither the divinity of Jesus nor the redemption of man's sins through the crucifixion made sense to me. While the Hindu gods can be rather confusing to a Western mind raised in monotheism, the idea of reincarnation appealed to me. It provided partial answers to what otherwise remained inexplicable. Given the enormity of the crimes committed and of the suffering caused, no human justice could redress the balance. The one assumption I made was that life had to make sense.

After rejecting my childish concept of God during that Sabbath service in Switzerland, I decided that we don't need rules issued by a divine authority; we could follow the humanism of the 18th century philosophers as a guide to ethical behavior. (This is pretty much were most Unitarians are today.) This freed us from rules that no longer made any sense.

Only it was not enough. I still had to come to terms with the Holocaust. In addition to Eastern thought, my studies contributed to opening my eyes. The order and vastness of the universe, the parallel between the microcosm and the macrocosm, the continuum of life from mineral to plant, from plant to animal and from animal to human led me to see intelligence at work, a nurturing of life in all its forms, an infinity that I, who had trouble with simple math problems, could not begin to fathom. I now recognized a divine force manifesting throughout the universe. Just like the sun shines on the good and the bad, just like the rain falls on the fields of the good and the bad, so this creative energy was the same for everyone, Christians and Jews, Moslems or Buddhists, good men and evil ones. I concluded that we came from the same divine life force and that made us all brothers.

Another important insight came from the short story "Colomba" by Prosper Mérimée, the author of *Carmen*. Colomba takes place in Corsica and describes an ongoing feud between two families—typical tribal behavior: one from column A kills one from column B, and one from column B kills one from Column A until there is no one left to kill. I saw where hatred and revenge lead and decided that I had the power to stop the hatred with me: I did not have to return hatred with hatred. That insight, coupled with my conviction that life had to make sense and that the universe was just, allowed me to let go of the hate. I could leave it up to the universe to somehow restore the balance. The need to bring perpetrators to justice, however imperfect, remained because we want to live in an orderly civil society under the rule of law.

I still don't have an explanation or even an understanding as to why the Holocaust had to happen, any more than I understand the killing fields of Cambodia, the butchery of Yugoslavia and all the other killings that continue into the 21st century. But for me this insight allowed me to get on with my own life.

As we got closer to the exam, Mlle. Noyon pinned our hopes on the literary dissertation. For an entire month I wrote a composition every day under exam conditions: I was given a topic, a blank sheet of paper and three hours.

Because the French published the topics of compositions given at the *Baccalauréat* in previous years, there was an ample supply of topics available. One was, "History justifies anything we want according to Voltaire." Another topic was a paragraph from a sermon by Bossuet wherein he vigorously defended the absolute monarchy by divine right of King Louis XIV. Did Bossuet defend the absolute monarchy so strongly because he knew it was on its way out?

And so, by the time exam day arrived, writing a paper had become second nature. The written exam took two days. Three hours were for writing the composition, three hours for math and three hours to translate a piece about an ante-diluvian animal from English to French and a three-hour German translation. I did well.

Once you passed the written exam you faced orals in French, English, math, history and geography. Since there was no time to study history that year, I managed to get a medical deferment to take the exam in the fall. I was truly exhausted and the excuse was not faked. It gave me the summer to bone up on history.

Vacations for young people in those days were segregated: workers went on their vacations and students went through the Office of University Tourism. Since I had left-leaning views, I idealized blue-collar workers and chose to go to an inexpensive camp for young workers for two weeks. Though I was poorer than most of my fellow campers, they rejected me. It was a painful experience. The only other student in the camp and I ended up spending most of our time together talking and playing lots of ping-pong.

When I got back to Toulouse, Mlle. Noyon gave me a massive tongue lashing for not studying enough. After that, I buckled down. At the oral in September I did well in English—they thought I had a good pronunciation. I boned up on my math theorems and did a competent *explication de texte* (analysis of a text). Though I had studied my history, results were poor compared to my other grades. The material was new to me, so I couldn't distinguish between important events or major trends and secondary ones. I remembered details without getting on top of the whole picture. Happily, I passed. The following year I went to the Lycée de Jeunes Filles in Toulouse to prepare for the second *Baccalauréat*. I had achieved the seemingly impossible. Mme. Brun shared in my triumph and remained very encouraging. By that time, however, Mlle. L. had moved to Caen and we lost touch.

I did not have the same depth of knowledge as someone who had completed six years of *lycée* because I didn't have as much reading under my belt. Nevertheless, I acquired skills and the ability to think things through. Often it felt as though someone had pried my head open and inserted a wealth of knoweledge and ideas. But even more important, I had learned how to think and reason—I could now figure things out for myself. It felt wonderful. In addition, as I continued to study, I stopped having the sense of being buffeted by others. Perhaps I was not as stupid as I had previously thought because I knew that getting my *Baccalauréat* was quite an achievement.

Denise Noyon had become the dominant figure in my life; I idolized her. She changed my life by taking on the challenge of helping me earn my degree under incredible circumstances. When it was all over she said she would never again help anyone make up five or six years of schooling in one—she would need at least two years. She knew she'd pushed me to the limit and beyond.

She also helped me cope with my mother. Under Mlle. Noyon's influence, I learned to remain calm, leave the apartment and not return until my mother had calmed down on her own. Sometimes that could take as long as 20 or 30 minutes. She told me I was intelligent, that I was to accomplish important things and that to do so I had to isolate myself and stay away from people. This advice was constant and runs like a theme through my diary. I accepted everything she said as if it were Gospel truth.

Mlle. Noyon came from a very conservative, French Catholic family from Lille. Her family had aristocratic roots, she claimed, but they had dropped the *particule*, the *de* that denotes aristocracy. As time went on, I came to believe that her parents disliked Jews. She lived with her parents in a house where two rooms had been set aside for her school. In order to earn enough money, she did bookkeeping after school was out.

On the day after my mother locked me out, I'd gone to school without breakfast. She sat me down in her little yard and brought me coffee and some bread. She asked me to speak in a low voice so that her parents wouldn't hear. She was feeding me behind their backs, and I thought it was because I was Jewish—which was strange, since several of her students were Jewish and she was paid by a Jewish social service agency. Besides, this was post-war Europe and everyone had seen where antisemitism had led.

She also said she was clairvoyant and into psychic phenomena. To enhance my ability to perform academically, she would frequently "hypnotize" me. I always remained conscious of what she was doing, she never made any suggestions that I was not comfortable with, and I always remembered what she said. She would have me relax on her bed. To speed things up she would apply pressure under my brow bone near the bridge of the nose. I was never out. She calmed me down and relaxed me, especially to help me cope with my mother. She also fed me suggestions via the Coué method, to help me with my schoolwork. (Coué developed a method of conscious autosuggestion that was dependent on the routine repetition of expressions, such as my own "My mind is clear....)

Some of her contributions to my life were less positive. As a clairvoyant, she often helped physicians diagnose illnesses. (In those days we did not have the ability to look inside the body as we do today.) Now that I understand a bit more about clairvoyance, I know that it is not 100 percent foolproof. But at the time, I was led to believe that it was as clear as normal vision.

A series of incidents should have opened my eyes. Once, upon arriving at school, she told me that I had made a flippant remark to some people in the outdoor market about my Jewishness. This was untrue and totally out of character for me. After years of persecution, the last thing I would have done would be to assert my Jewishness. But instead of asking where she got this information, I assumed that someone had badmouthed me. In fact, it must have been something she had "seen" or "picked up," given her preconceived notions.

Another day, she told me that some Jewish students had sent a fire truck to her house; on a different occasion it was an ambulance. This frightened her aging parents half to death. I believed that, too. There were more stories along the same lines. She expressed a great deal of anger and hostility toward the Jewish students she accused of doing this to her. Now I realize she must have imagined it all. She probably was not lying, but recounting visions rather than actual events. She probably saw images that corresponded to her preconceived notions.

Among the things Mlle. Noyon introduced me to were the lives of saints. I read the story of St. Teresa of Avila, but could not relate to her strict asceticism, nor could I ever accept the idea that the suffering of one person could relieve the suffering of another. St. Teresa would walk and endure pain in order to relieve the suffering of the missionaries in Africa. That did not make sense to me.

She also gave me the biography of Le St. Curé d'Ars, a priest who was into poltergeists and other supernatural phenomena. He instilled in me the belief that dancing was sinful, and I, who so loved to dance, refrained from doing so in deference to his teaching. Once, my mother dragged me to a Purim ball where I met some old friends. One of them invited me to dance. I did not refuse, but I was so stiff to the point where he asked me if something was wrong.

Finally, Mlle. Noyon gave me *The Rosicrucian Cosmo-Conception* by Max Heindel. It was for initiates and dealt with esoteric teachings and mystical Christianity. This big book was written at the end of the 19th century and drew on Christian mysticism from the medieval period. I discovered for the first time that Christians accused Jews of killing their "Savior." It also reflected the racist ideas that led to the Holocaust. Needless to say, Jews were presented badly. The book had a negative impact on me. I was not equipped to deal with these accusations and it was certainly not what I needed under the circumstances. It made me feel guilty and I even apologized mentally, though I had no idea whether these accusations were true or false. At any rate, it made no sense to me to punish people for things that were done 2,000 years ago.

At the time, however, my devotion to her was absolute. In my eyes she could do no wrong. She had done so much for me; she had turned my whole life around, mostly for the better. Besides, there was no one else to talk to or to provide a counterweight to my experiences. Because of our close relationship, I kept in touch with her even after I moved to the U.S. At one point she was desperate for money and I sent her some. I thought of it as a partial repayment for tuition.

In 1956, when my husband and I went to France, I visited her in Lille. She told me that she felt bad that she could not pay me back. Instead, she gave me a gold ring with four small diamonds. Eventually, she married an old friend from her youth who had become a widower. And that was the last letter I got from her.

On a subsequent visit to Toulouse I ran into Michele, one of the other students she had been very close to after I left her school. To my great surprise Michele did not speak highly of her. She indicated that Mlle Noyon did not have all her marbles. Gradually it dawned on me that she may have been right.

With Mlle. Noyon.
(The photo was taken in 1956 when I visited her in Lille.)

TOULOUSE III
September 1947 - September 1949:
The Baccalauréat

I was accepted into the Lycée des Jeunes Filles in Toulouse. Most of my classmates were just a year younger than I, nice girls, mostly middle- to upper middle-class, many from well-to-do families. At that time, France's secular public schools were reputed to be better than its religious schools, so they attracted good students. Besides, the first *Baccalauréat* also weeded out the less able students.

Though I had sought to get into a specific philosophy professor's class, I did not get the professor I wanted. The woman I ended up with was conscientious, but pedestrian, though she did have a reputation of getting students through the *Baccalauréat*. She believed religion was a crutch and a weakness. I felt that, as a philosophy professor, she should have thought things through.

Her job was to get us to pass the exam, and so, most of the time she lectured. During breaks she did not speak to students in order to save her voice. In spite of this, she was our most important instructor because we spent 11 hours with her every week. We studied philosophy, psychology, ethics, sociology and metaphysics. We read Descartes' *Discourse on the Method* and Plato's *Phaedo*. For this course I picked up a second-hand philosophy textbook, one that was used by parochial schools. This turned out to be a mistake on my part as the teacher vetoed it since it was not on the approved list of textbooks. (Because of my financial situation, I could not afford to buy another one.)

Classe de Philosophie, Lycée de Jeunes Filles.
I'm in the back row on the right.

In math we did some calculus and astronomy. I was fascinated by the subject since it opened up the immensity of the universe and gave me a new perspective of life on earth. Botany and biology were fascinating and became subjects I came to love. I loved biology so much that I thought of studying medicine, but even I realized that was an unattainable goal. Our finances simply did not permit that.

We covered plant and human anatomy and physiology, but without touching on the reproductive system, even though most girls were between the ages of 17 and 20 and should have been informed. (Instead, on Thursday mornings, they offered us a class in child care where we were taught how to bathe an infant.) We also studied physics and chemistry, my first exposure to both subjects.

We had some lab work in biology and I was so excited when I looked through a microscope and saw the individual cells on a thin layer of onion skin. It was through my biology class that I learned about proper nutrition, part of learning all about the human body and its needs. Afterward, I became more selective in what I ate. We also kept up with French literature and with English.

History and geography deserve special mention. Our professor was a short, stocky woman in her 30s with a pug nose and large, horn-rimmed glasses. The students made fun of her and she was unable to maintain discipline. The girls threw spitballs in her presence or they brought their stockings to mend during class. But she was an excellent teacher and I used to sit up front so I could hear her lecture. In geography we covered the great economic powers including the U.S., the British Empire and the USSR. I discovered a real love of history and I tied for first or second place with another student in that subject.

The philosophers who came up with systems and answers to explain the riddle of our existence fascinated me, and I was disappointed when critics found flaws in their world views. To me, the course was more than a required subject, it was an attempt to answer my burning questions about the meaning of life. I threw myself into the subject and received good grades on the twice-monthly dissertations we had to submit. I eventually won second prize in the subject.

At the end of the year, I also received two lesser awards, one for English and one for physics. Imagine my surprise when I failed my second *Baccalauréat.* But there was no recourse. I planned to take the exam again in the fall.

Financially, that year was tough. Though the scholarship was extended for a second year, it was not increased in spite of France's raging inflation. To make matters worse, my mother was frequently without a job. At one point we had nothing to eat and I would go to school hungry. I hit upon the idea of stopping at the Jewish children's home for lunch. We received a C.A.R.E. package from Aunt Anny in the U.S. and I left what little food there was for my mother.

I did not allow myself to go anywhere that summer. The possibility of failing the exam was so threatening that I stayed home and studied 12 hours a day. In Toulouse the weather can get very hot and humid. That summer I started to get headaches. Did I stop studying? No. Instead, I put a wet washcloth on my forehead and continued my work. Again, I flunked. With four hours to write a philosophical dissertation, my mind went blank. I was exhausted.

It was a disaster. Now what? I wanted to continue and try again the following spring, but my scholarship was not renewed. My mother did not know what to do. She went to Mlle. Noyon who told her that I should be allowed to try again. She agreed to take me on for free, every day for half a day. The other half of the day I worked for a Spanish woman as a seamstress apprentice. My mother wanted me to have some way of making a living, but I received no pay from the seamstress, and she wasn't teaching me to make garments, either. I put up many hems and sewed on lots of buttons but nothing that would prepare me for making an independent living. What the seamstress did do was to make some clothes for us during the off season at no charge.

It would be another tough year under Mlle. Noyon and her psychic influences. She told me to befriend Anne-Marie and encouraged me to stay away from other people in order to realize my future potential. My diary is full of her exhortations. Anne-Marie, nicknamed Maitou, was four years younger than I. She was very pretty, always well-dressed and from a well-to-do family. She was very bright and we enjoyed talking, but our life experiences were miles apart.

Once, we were asked to sing something in class. She sang a little song about a girl who was a disappointment to her family because they already had two girls and they had hoped for a boy, but her little cousin made up for that. Maitou was praised to the skies. When my turn came I sang the "Ode to Joy." Mlle. Noyon's reaction? "Yeah, you sing to pitch." That's all I got. With the power she had over me, that was the end of my singing.

I finally passed the written and oral exams in June 1949. I still remember the topic of my paper. We had to discuss the rights of the city or community versus the rights of the individual. The proper approach was of course to debate the views of famous philosophers before reaching a conclusion. Many of us were concerned that the professors who graded our papers might be Communists, so we had to tread lightly, at least we thought so.

I never again flunked an exam. I became very disciplined and organized, often denying myself even simple pleasures in order to be prepared. Above all, I learned to walk into an exam fresh, alert and fully rested.

By the summer of 1949, my mother and I were desperate. She was working, but her earnings were not enough for the two of us. I could not find anything. France's economy had not recovered from the war and jobs were scarce. I went to Mr. Levy, a member of the Consistoire (the Jewish communal organization) in Toulouse. He told me that the newly-hired young rabbi from North Africa and his wife had just had a baby and she needed someone to help her around the house. When I went to see her, she refused to give me the job because, she said, she could not order me to wash the floor since I had the *Baccalauréat*. I pleaded with her, but to no avail. She would not hire me.

I went back to Mr. Levy who told me about a Jewish merchant, a Mr. Finkel, who needed a sales girl. Mr. Finkel traveled to the *foires*, the outdoor markets, and every day would be in a different town. I took the job. It was backbreaking. Every morning we left Toulouse between 5 and 6 A.M. and traveled for one and-a-half or two hours to our destination. Then we unpacked the van, set up our table, pitched the overhead tent, laid out our wares and were ready for business by 9 A.M.

I was on my feet all day, except for a brief 20- or 30-minute rest at lunch. We had a wicker trunk upon which Mr. Finkel would sit, but I was almost never allowed to sit on it. "The trunk cannot support two people," he claimed. Or, "It's better not to sit because if you then get up that chases the customer away." So I was on my feet for 12 hours every day. On the heavy days of my period it was murder.

Around 6 P.M. we packed up our stuff and loaded the van. This usually took two hours, and then it was time for the trip home. I rarely got home before 10 P.M., more often 11. I would fall into bed exhausted only to start all over again the next day.

On occasion we would go to a more distant town where there were only one or two big market days every year. Then we had to stay in some small hotel. The shepherds wearing black smocks and broad-rimmed hats would come down from the Pyrénées, walking with their herds of sheep. They sold their animals at 4 or 5 A.M., ate breakfast, and by 8 A.M. were ready to shop for clothes, tools and other necessities. These market days were similar to our county fairs except

Working on the *foires*, the outdoor markets, with Mr. Finkel. Summer, 1949.

that there was real merchandise available in addition to farm products and amusement park rides.

One time, Mr. Finkel neglected to reserve two rooms for us and there was no other room to be had. Of course, he took the room for himself. I slept in the back of a truck filled with hardware with only a canvas separating me from the street. There were revelers in the street and at one point a street fight broke out. I did not dare stick my head out, nor did I sleep much that night.

Mr. Finkel considered Sundays a half-day. I worked from 7 A.M. until 1 or 2 P.M. in Toulouse at the Place St. Sernin. The problem with Sundays was that there was no public transportation because the streetcars did not run. I had a one-hour walk to get to the square and another hour walk to get home. By the time I got home, I was too exhausted to do anything but sleep. During the entire summer I did not crack a book or go out. Nor is there a single entry in my diary during those three months.

For some reason, Mr. Finkel never picked me up at home. Instead, he asked me to wait for him on a bridge at a crossroad near the canal, about 20 minutes walking distance from my house. One time he was very late. It was 6 A.M. and I was getting chilly. So I put on the sweater I carried in my bag along with a handkerchief and my *Carte d'Identité*. As I took off my jacket to put on the sweater, a policeman approached and rudely asked me what I was doing. I told him about my sweater. Still rude, he asked for my profession. He looked incredulous when I told him I was a student. By then I figured out that he had taken me for a prostitute.

"Do you have ID?" he asked. I pulled out my card that showed that I was a student. His demeanor softened. "What are you doing here?" he wanted to know. I explained that I was waiting for my *patron*, my boss, who was late and I was pacing because I was cold. He left, satisfied, but not without keeping an eye on me. I like to tell the story as one of the high points of my life.

In 1949 there were still a lot of Germans in France, POWs working in France as part of WWII reparations. After four or five years they were allowed to go home. Before leaving, they would shop. Goods were abundant in France by 1949 and even the quality was improving. My knowledge of German came in handy. A German POW came to buy some underwear from our stand. By the time he left I had sold him two shirts, a sweater and a suit in addition to his underwear. Mr. Finkel was very pleased. Instead of some desperately need cash, however, my bonus was a box of pastries.

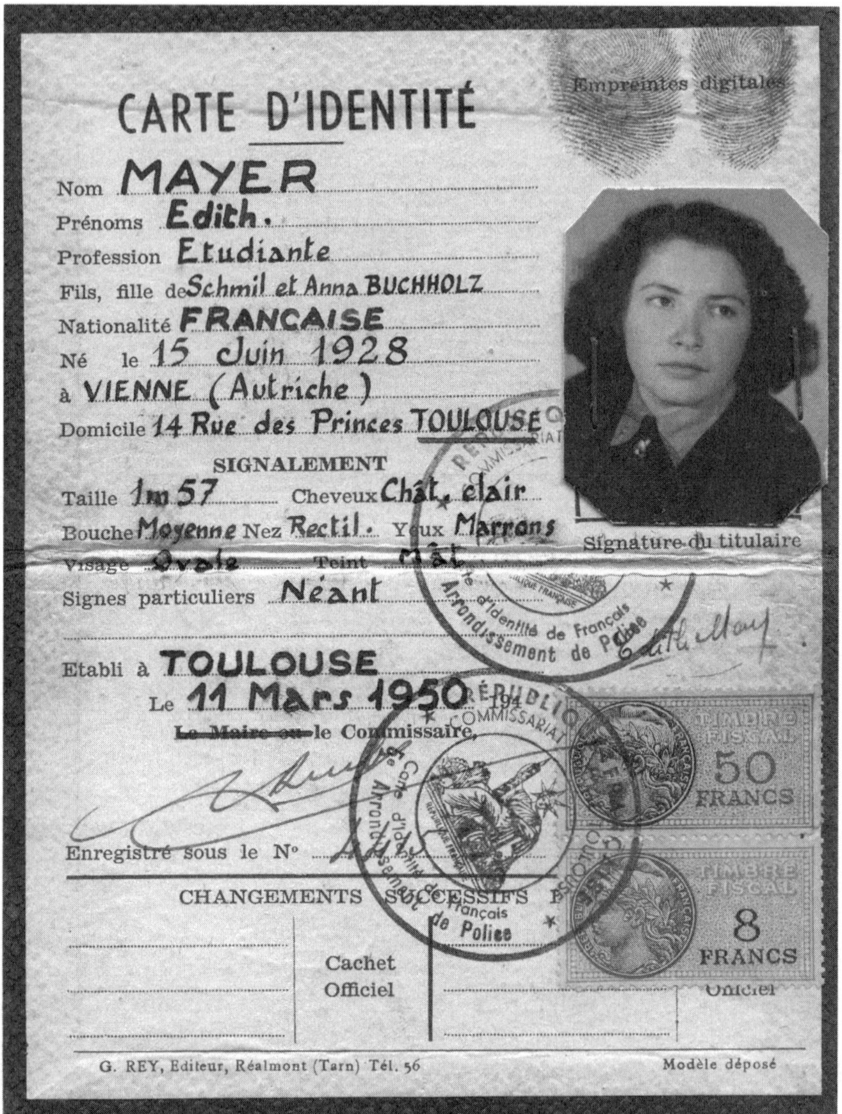

CARTE D'IDENTITÉ

Empreintes digitales

Nom MAYER

Prénoms Edith.

Profession Etudiante

Fils, fille de Schmil et Anna BUCHHOLZ

Nationalité FRANCAISE

Né le 15 Juin 1928

à VIENNE (Autriche)

Domicile 14 Rue des Princes TOULOUSE

SIGNALEMENT

Taille 1m 57 Cheveux Chât. clair

Bouche Moyenne Nez Rectil. Yeux Marrons

Visage Ovale Teint Mât

Signes particuliers Néant

Signature du titulaire

Etabli à TOULOUSE

Le 11 Mars 1950

~~Le Maire ou~~ le Commissaire,

Enregistré sous le N°

CHANGEMENTS SUCCESSIFS

Cachet Officiel

TIMBRE FISCAL 50 FRANCS

TIMBRE FISCAL 8 FRANCS

G. REY, Editeur, Réalmont (Tarn) Tél. 56 — Modèle déposé

My *Carte d'Identité.*

Mr. Finkel was anything but generous. He paid me FF7,000. When I left to go to school he paid my replacement FF12,000. That hurt. When I asked why he answered, "Because you live with your mother." Didn't he know that we were in dire financial straights? In my naïveté I did not think that anyone would take advantage of me to such an extent, especially one Jew to another. He had a wife and a teenage son who never helped his father out. Needless to say, Mr. Finkel exploited me mercilessly.

Toward the end of the summer he made a pass at me. I was not interested. On top of that I made fun of his big hands. He was hurt. And that was the end of that.

My mother was heavily criticized for allowing me to work at this kind of a job. "For this you let her study?" they asked. At that time in France "nice girls did not do this." I told her the fable about the miller, his son and the donkey in which people always find fault, no matter who is or is not riding the donkey. That story made her feel better.

Throughout this time my mother was pushing me to get married. Though I was 21 years old, the last thing on my mind was marriage. In my diary I discovered that one of her motivations was to help me find a man of some means so that she wouldn't have to work. She did not have my best interests at heart, especially since she knew that I sacrificed so much in order to be able to study.

I had my math oral on a Friday. The next morning, Saturday, I was in Cahors at the market when the math professor who had tested me the day before walked by. He looked at me absolutely incredulous. "This could not possibly be the same girl" was clearly written across his face. He did not stop and I did not say anything.

One man regularly came to the markets and stood out more than the others. He looked like an intellectual, with snow white hair, sensitive features and diaphanous skin. He clearly did not belong. It turned out he was a Quaker and a vegetarian who came to the *foires* to help his wife who was Jewish. During the war he had hidden her. She owed him her life and married him after the war. He invited me to join him to get together with some "friends." At the time I did not know that he meant Quakers, as I took the word in its ordinary meaning. I never did meet with his "friends," though I always enjoyed talking to him.

Mr. Finkel didn't start out as a *forain*. He had an engineering degree in agronomy. Before the war he represented Massey Harris and sold agricultural machinery. But the war turned everyone's life upside down, so there he was trying to get back on his feet. And he was not alone. The markets attracted a motley assortment of people.

Recently, on a trip to France, I stopped at a market in Toulouse to see what it was like. The market was the same, though some of the merchandise had changed. But the most drastic change was in the people who were staffing the booths: Lots of people were from former French colonies in Africa and the West Indies. There were a few Frenchmen, some Hispanics, some people from the Middle East and even some Indians.

I must have been good at selling because at the end of the summer Mr. Finkel offered to equip me with a van and merchandise to go out and sell on my own. I said no. I was determined to finish my education.

LA FACULTÉ DE LETTRES
1949 -1952: At the University

When I found out that I had passed my second *Baccalauréat* I was overjoyed. I applied to the Faculté de Lettres. With excitement I ran up and down the empty hallways that summer, noticing the names of the classrooms, inhaling the smell of the old building, and checking out the large amphitheatre. I was like a little kid in a candy store. It was a dream come true.

I looked forward to the start of school. There was a formal, solemn return to classes for all the schools of the University of Toulouse marked with a ceremony called *Commencement*. It was comparable to American convocation ceremonies and included distinguished speakers. I got very confused when I came to America where graduation exercises were also called commencement, which literally means beginning!

At the commencement ceremony that marked the opening of the school year, three honorary degrees were awarded. The recipients were Charles Morgan, an English author whose novels I had read in translation and admired a great deal; an Italian scientist and a Belgian economist. In my diary I refer to it as one of the most beautiful days of my life; I was supremely happy with its intellectual atmosphere.

At the ceremony I chatted with a sophisticated young woman who sat next to me. Her name was Aline, and she became a close friend throughout my student years. We saw a great deal of each other. She was a philosophy major and we often exchanged notes in our search for the meaning of life.

Finances were still a problem. I did not have to pay the usual fees except for a library and an infirmary fee. By then the French government had accepted some responsibility for the deportations, so I became *une pupille de la nation* (a ward of the nation), as if my father had been killed on the battlefield. The scholarship was minimal (6,000 old francs), not enough to live on. To make matters worse, it was not paid out until January though classes began in early November. As a result, I would hang out at the social services office to beg for jobs or an advance of coupons for the subsidized student restaurant.

I gave my mother all the money I earned during the summer at the outdoor markets and my scholarship money. For books and personal expenses I relied on the little money I earned tutoring.

I tutored everyone and everything. Denise Noyon had me come to her school to teach German. I prepared a girl for her entrance exam to the Post Office, mostly arithmetic and geography. I tutored Vietnamese students preparing for the entrance exam to one of the *Grandes Ecoles*, the equivalent of our Ivy League schools. I tutored a neighbor girl who was preparing for the *Certificat d'Etudes*, even though she was a hopeless case. I remember doing a translation from German to French on schizophrenia. I did whatever I could find and never turned down a legitimate job.

In school I had to work twice as hard as the others. Given the speed with which I had rushed through the classics, I had often only read a summary of the works and not the full text. This left no time for a social life. My mother warned me that I had to choose between going to the university or my wardrobe. Of course I chose school. Once I was invited to a Christmas dinner. All the women wore dressy cocktail outfits while I wore my navy blue skirt, a blouse and a navy sweater, the same clothes I wore to school every day.

Because of my study schedule, there was no time or money for sports, though I still took my breaks on Sunday morning with a walk or a swim in the Garonne. Once the river became polluted, I swam at the pool, or took a canoe trip, usually alone.

I was thrilled to be in school but had a difficult time narrowing down my choice of major. My first love was psychology, so in my first year at the *faculté* I attended both my required courses and psych classes. I could not keep it up because certain classes were reserved for majors. I found out early on that I could not have gotten a degree in psychology without spending a year in Paris because experimental psychology was not offered in Toulouse. I knew that this was beyond our means, and so I dropped it.

My second love was history. I took a lot of history classes and did well. One of the professors urged me to choose it as a major. When I told him about some of my other interests he advised me to first get a degree in history, then I could do the other course work. That was out of the question since I didn't have the necessary financial resources to stay in school that long.

It took a minimum of four years to get a *Licence-es-Lettres*. Many students took longer. I couldn't, for we were starving, our living conditions were primitive, and life with mother was stressful. To get a degree in a foreign language the school required a one-year stay abroad in the country of the target language. I knew I could avoid that since I already had native fluency in German. So I chose German first with English as a second language and a French literature minor. That shaved one year off my course of study, assuming I could pass two major exams each year.

The French had started to experiment with the curriculum. That year they introduced a preparatory year in an attempt to bring their system more in line with the Anglo-Saxon model. The year was called "*Propédeutique*." Instead of plunging into a major, we all had to take additional general courses covering the 18th and the 19th centuries in depth. We covered literature, history, art, music and architecture, looking at those two centuries from all angles. The courses were taught by professors from different disciplines. Though it was a lot of work, it was also very exciting because, for the first time, a whole picture began to emerge. All those little facts we had committed to memory for the *Baccalauréat* fell into place like the pieces of a giant jig-saw puzzle. Suddenly you could see the sweep of history. Many years later, when I said this to one of my colleagues in the history department in Pennsylvania, he said most American students never get to that point—they never get to see the whole picture.

The French university system is very different from that of American colleges and universities. It is a cross between American graduate schools and independent study. Lectures were given in the large amphitheatre that held 100 to 200 students, with little opportunity to meet the professors. Assignments were published in a monthly bulletin we bought at special bookstores that catered to the needs of university students.

Our social lives, housing, emotional or spiritual needs were of no concern to the academy. There was no football team or other collegiate sports. The Dean of the *Faculté de Lettres* was a professor with a reduced load. He was assisted by two secretaries. That was it. The small social service office was in a separate location and met the needs of all the schools in the area: medicine, pharmacy, engineering, law and so on. Students were left to their own devices. There were no *in loco parentis* concerns. You were free to attend classes or not. Classes for each course were given once a week, and only part of the material was covered in class. The rest was left for independent, unsupervised study though students had to hand in monthly research papers for each subject, or lengthy translations for the language departments. Exams were held only once, at the end of the year, so you could goof off most of the time, then cram at the end. To succeed in this system, you needed a great deal of self-discipline.

There were often requests to share our class notes with fellow students who were far from the campus. I typed notes in the school's office, using my own class notes and those of a fellow student. The office mimeographed them and I sent them out. I spent lots of time doing that—for free of course. Because of this work, I developed friendships with two young men, one a would-be military career officer who was in Spain at the time. The other was in Tunisia. I briefly dated his brother, a medical student in Toulouse, but I never let the fellow in Tunisia know that.

In the fall, the freshmen organized an outing. We rented a bus, packed a picnic lunch and took off to the nearby Pyrénées. We had so much fun that a second outing was planned. I remember staying home the second time because of work and study pressures. I often think about that sacrifice because I wanted so much to go, yet I felt duty bound to stay behind and study.

For me the university provided the first casual interaction with members of the opposite sex. While I did not date, we often did things as a group, especially in the German Department. One of us would volunteer to buy tickets to a Wagnerian opera or a concert for the whole group, and we would all go together. We also had a social every year where the professor briefly honored us with his presence. I was elected treasurer of the German Language Club. I somehow knew who had money and who didn't, and this was kept quiet when it came to paying dues. For our annual party there was money for champagne for the professor, with wine, soft drinks and cookies for everyone else.

In the spring of my first year, one of my classmates, Huguette, lost her father. Her mother died when she was 3 and her grandparents helped raise her. I had much empathy for her, having lost Papa and

Huguette and I, university students. Spring 1952.

Kurt. We ended up becoming close friends. Every summer I was invited to visit her home in Cahors and her grandparents' country house. She was very wealthy, yet she complained of boredom. I found that incomprehensible because I always had more books to read than I had time for. She was a good Catholic, but that did not interfere with our friendship.

For me those two weeks in Cahors were a novel experience. I ate very well and I did not have to work. Her grandparents had a full-time maid and the dinner table conversation was interesting. I was introduced to her extended family, characters all. They took over the estate of French aristocrats at the time of the French Revolution. It was my introduction to what we called *la vieille France*.

Huguette benefited greatly from our friendship because I helped her with her papers. I would proofread her monthly dissertation and her German translations and would make needed corrections. After her father died, her grandparents did not allow her to spend the week in Toulouse, where she had a room in a boarding house run by nuns. She now had to live at home and traveled to Toulouse only once a week for classes.

Huguette and I did not share the same vision of life. She told me I aimed too high and risked falling down with a crash. What brought this on was a conversation in which I used the word *absolute* and in which I touched on current problems, talked about great men, my interest in culture and my reaction to tradition. Huguette countered that her goal was a quiet, peaceful life where people should not be too demanding.

Of course Huguette was raised by her grandparents in a Victorian manner. With the family's daily five- or six-course lunches that lasted for two hours, Huguette was overweight and not very active. She was very attached to her wealth, her money, to the pleasures of the table and to her comfort. I concluded that trying to convince her to pursue other goals was a waste of time. As a result, I decided not to bring up my concerns and my dreams and to limit myself to more superficial exchanges.

Based on the entry in my diary, I responded to her initial invitation in order to study, coach her in German, get some exercise and maybe even have a party. None of this materialized. In addition to that, I was a vegetarian at that time and I avoided alcohol. So at every meal her grandmother gave me grief. In spite of all that, we remained friends through the years and even corresponded after I left for the United States.

When I returned to Cahors in 1956 after my marriage, she felt I had become too "American" and broke off our friendship. She married late, had only one daughter who was still single at the age of 40, and was widowed early. My attempt to reconnect with her was unsuccessful.

During my student years I met students from Muslim countries, mostly from Algeria and Morocco, later from Iran. I became friendly with some of them. I was only vaguely aware of political events as I had no radio and I did not read the newspapers. While my contacts with the Arab students were superficial, this was held against me by some Jewish students, especially those from North Africa. Of course I should have been more aware of Israel's struggle for survival.

At the same time I am glad to have had these contacts as this sort of casual interaction becomes more difficult once we are adults ensconced in our respective milieus. What struck me most about the Arabs were their wide mood swings, almost to the point of being manic-depressive. They were not practicing Muslims, they ignored Ramadan, consumed alcohol and enjoyed casual interaction with French girls, well aware that they would have to give it up once they were back home. Ready or not, all wanted independence for Algeria.

I also met a student from India, nicknamed Maxi. He was from Pondicherry, a one-time French town on the southeast coast of India. He was Catholic and made fun of my interest in eastern religions. I thought he was a brilliant young man. He studied both law and Latin and could get away with preparing his exams in just the last two months of the school year. It was a purely platonic friendship, but we were very close, walking together and exchanging long letters when he was in Paris.

My love life was non-existent. Except for the casual contacts at school, in the student restaurant and at the library, I did not date. There are long monologues in my diary about that. I wanted male companionship, perhaps even more than just companionship, and then I would berate myself for wanting that. One entry that makes me smile today says that at least it proves that I am normal. But with the pressure to study for the exams and pass them at the first try, plus work, there was no time for romance.

I should add that my appearance was probably not very attractive to young men. I looked like a kid, wore no make up or even lipstick, and was badly dressed. My mother had received a small amount of money from someone in Germany? Austria? France? I really don't know. What did she do with that money? Instead of buying me something nice to wear, she went out and bought third-rate kitchen towels! The quality was inferior, stiff and non-absorbent, as fabrics had yet to reach prewar quality, but her concern was that I did not have a dowry. Such were her priorities.

Mail continued to be important for me. I got letters from Jacques, fewer from Leon. He was working as a counselor in a home for Jewish orphans. I found out later that he had a girlfriend. He didn't write often because of the many demands on his time. While it is true that he was not preparing his future—the job was a dead end job—his life was pleasant and carefree: He was a big hero to the children and his love-life was fulfilling. Once he asked me in a letter whether I was happy. I had to think before answering. My studies were the fulfillment of a dream, but life with my mother continued to be a major source of stress.

When school started, we were told that we had to buy "*des dictionnaires de Licence,*" English and German dictionaries for that level, and lots of other books. I did not have the needed money. These books were expensive and I had given my mother all the money I had earned during the summer.

At the time, my mother was working in a sweatshop in the budding garment industry in Toulouse. I decided to do piece work as well. Every day she brought home two coats that had to be hand finished: collar, lining, button holes, buttons. It would take me at least two hours for each coat. This lasted for about six or eight weeks until I earned enough money to buy the needed books. I never missed classes but did not do much studying during that period or get enough sleep. Healthy or sick you had to keep at it because once you took on the responsibility of doing the work, the coats had to be ready by the following morning.

During the rest of the school year I mostly tutored. For the next two summers I continued to work on the *foires* with a different employer. He paid a little better, allowed me to sit, but was unpleasant. A chemical engineer, originally from Russia, he was married to an attractive French woman and had three children. He, too, was trying get back on his feet after the disruption of the war. Like Mr. Finkel, he was Jewish, though his wife was not. On the *foires* the work was so exhausting that, again, I didn't crack a book all summer, nor is there a single entry in my diary.

Back in school, the Social Service Office referred me to the local branch of a well-known bookseller, the Librairie Joseph Gibert, to help out for three weeks in the fall. Since the *lycées* started about five weeks before the university, I had time to do that job. I would start at 8 A.M. and work until 8 P.M. with one hour off for lunch. I remember that I needed to rest my feet at lunchtime, but I could not afford a restaurant, so I went to a newly-opened ice cream parlor called the Igloo where I had a *Café Liégeois,* cold coffee with ice cream topped with whipped cream. That was my lunch. I knew it was not a healthy diet, but I had to sit down and it was delicious, cheap and nearby.

The manager liked me and invited me back for the next two years, until I left for the States. He told me that I was a good sales girl. When I expressed surprise, he said: "Didn't anyone tell you that?" Well, no one did. I should have guessed, though, because both of my previous employers had offered to set me up with a van and merchandise if I would go out and sell for them on the *foires*.

One day M. Crouzet, one of my professors, walked into the bookstore. I still remember the incredulous look on his face when he saw me. He asked, "What are you doing here, Mlle. Mayer?" I felt like answering, "What does it look like?" but I didn't. The fact is that, at that time, university students did not take jobs below their status. What is routine in America was unheard of in France.

My choice of studies at the Faculté was geared toward a greater understanding of what happened during the war. By studying German I hoped to find an explanation as to how that country, that culture which was part of my own, could do such a thing. But my professors, Mlle. Runacher and M. Boyer, were of little help. She had been a high school teacher whose methods were geared to the *lycée* and her lectures lacked depth.

M. Boyer was a Germanophile. He was old, loved music (the title of his doctoral thesis was *The Romanticism of Beethoven*), and neither the subject of antisemitism in German literature nor the horrors of Nazi Germany were discussed. There was a brief mention of Father Jahn's rabid antisemitism in his *Burschenschaften* (fraternal gymnastic associations) at the beginning of the 19th century, and that was it. The virulent antisemitism of the German Romantics, the long red thread of antisemitism throughout German history—starting with Luther and culminating with the racist ideas of the 19th century—were things I learned much later on my own.

M. Boyer was not helpful in my academic studies either. While I received above average grades in his classes, he denied me the top grades. There was another girl in our class whose father had been a diplomat in Switzerland. She had the benefit of first-rate schooling and an excellent command of German. She got the French equivalent of A's. She was arrogant and well aware of her privileged status. Once, as we climbed the stairs to the amphitheater side by side for our lecture class, we walked on either side of a hand rail in the middle of the stairs. She turned to me and said, "There is more than this handrail separating us." At the time I didn't realize what she was talking about, such was my naïveté.

In his tests M. Boyer tried to "catch" you, something I remembered later when I became a professor. I used tests as a learning device, always giving students ample notice as to what the test would cover. He did not. Toward the end of my studies at the Faculté, still insecure and unsure of my abilities, I asked him whether he thought I was good enough to try for the *Agrégation,* the diploma of distinction for those entering the upper echelons of education. He wouldn't tell me. All he said was "we'll see." Later, after working in New York, I wrote him that the Americans considered me an expert in German. He wrote back, "I should hope so." It would have been nice had he said that sooner.

During my last year at the Faculté, I got a job teaching German in a private school. Le Collège de Ligny was a Protestant boarding school for high school students. It was my first contact with Protestants, having always lived in Catholic countries. I was so used to being discriminated against that, during my interview, I asked the director whether the fact that I was Jewish would disqualify me for the job. He shrugged his shoulders and said, "Of course not." One of my fellow students who was a Protestant referred me to the job. He knew I worked during the school year, he didn't.

I spent Sunday afternoons and evenings preparing for classes, Monday morning I caught a bus at 7 A.M. After two hours I got off in Ligny and taught until 5 P.M. The bus brought me back to Toulouse at 7 P.M. I taught classes all day with a one-hour lunch break. The faculty was made up mostly of young couples with little children. I don't think they were paid very well, but out in the country, living conditions were pleasant. They were a very likeable bunch. Without the help of education courses I prepared for my classes and had a good academic year with the children. It also gave me practice in preparing lesson plans, something I had already done in the course of all the tutoring.

My scholarship had been increased to 12,000 old francs because I had passed all my exams. That money continued to go to my mother. The additional money I earned allowed me to buy my books and also some badly-needed clothes. One summer I owned only one summer dress, sent by Aunt Anny from America. It wasn't a bad-looking dress, pink with white polka dots, but I hated the polka dots. Summers are long in the south of France and I was very self-conscious to always be seen in the same dress. The following year I vowed that there would be no repeat performance. I went out and bought some fabric and made myself two simple dresses. I have a photograph of myself in one of them.

My housing situation with my mother continued to weigh heavily on me. It was so demeaning. I recall going to school, clenching my teeth and muttering under my breath, "I will not live like this, I will not live like this." The irony was that one of my neighbors was a blue-collar worker who was jealous of me. He told me, "I, too, would like to push the pen." What did he know of my struggles and sacrifices?

The housing situation also made studying very difficult. When my mother was home she loved to talk, preventing me from studying. She resented me for telling her "pretend that I am not home." But what was I to do? To read and take notes I went to the university library or the municipal library.

The municipal library was a new building, well-lit and warm in winter, with large tables where you could spread out your books and notes. While there was much traffic during the day, evenings were very quiet as the library was filled with students. The drawback was that I had to walk home, alone, late at night. I usually took back streets to get home more quickly. It was a brisk 30-minute walk. I always walked fast, well aware that the streets were not the safest place to be.

The libraries worked for studying, reading and note-taking, but not for writing research papers or preparing oral reports. For that I had to wait for the house to settle down and for my mother to go to bed. This was usually around 11 P.M. Then I would start working. That was the only way I could achieve full concentration and stay focused without interruptions. It meant staying up until the wee hours of the morning with the help of at least two cups of strong coffee.

On weekends it was my job to wash the floor in our tiny apartment. Noted in my diary is the observation that my mother would not do the dishes. She let them pile up in the sink for me to wash. Ditto for sheets and towels. In general, I was the man around the house, doing the heavy lifting, painting a kitchen cabinet and doing other chores. Laundry was left for breaks in the school year. I still took the laundry to the fountain up the street for rinsing and it was still an awful job, especially in the winter. But that was the least of my concerns. My mother continually pushed me to get married. Whenever I passed difficult exams, instead of sharing in my triumph, all she could say was, "She should only get married."

In reading my diary I discovered that she became cold and distant because I did not turn out to be the daughter she wanted. I was not like her. That was my biggest sin. And so, there was more rejection. My life was so full between my studies and my jobs. My mistake was that I still tried to love her and to please her.

The other much more serious problem was the lack of privacy. I had to hide my books, my diary and my correspondence from her. As a result I carried all these treasures around in my briefcase. There was one incident that almost drove me to madness. I recall thinking at the time that anyone can lose his mind given enough stress.

I continued to read and study *The Rosicrucian Cosmo-Conception*. Some of its suggestions were useful. One involved a daily five-minute concentration/meditation exercise in the morning and the other a review of the day in the evening. I had started a correspondence course. One Sunday Huguette had stopped for a visit. My books and notes were lying on the table when my mother discovered them. She went ballistic.

Of course our efforts to calm her down were in vain. Eventually, Huguette left. My mother continued to carry on, screaming I should give her all my "Christian" books. I lied and told her I had given everything to Huguette. That was not true. My stuff was still lying openly on the little table where I had barely rearranged the papers. It was like the story of Edgar Allan Poe's "Purloined Letter." The scene lasted for hours. Such outbursts would always leave her exhausted. Eventually she collapsed and went to bed, but the screaming, the threats, the insults left me in a terrible state, my stomach churning, my head spinning, ready to explode. I had had enough.

I could not take her any more. After all my efforts for years to stay calm, to be nice to her, to be compassionate, all seemed for naught. I was ready to leave home. I had my scholarship which had been increased, partly because of inflation, partly because I passed all my exams, two at a time, and I was earning a little money on the side. I knew I could manage on my own. What stopped me?

It was spring 1952, a few months before finals. As was my habit, I had taped my class schedule to the wall in the kitchen, next to my bed. That would have allowed her to find me. One evening, she even followed me to the municipal library. At one point, I was whispering to a friend sitting next to me and showing him some photos I had taken. When I looked up, guess who was standing behind me? My mother.

"So that's what you do at the library?" she cracked. I remember feeling deeply embarrassed. I knew that if I left home she would do the same thing and shame me in school. Being so close to my goal, I was not about to interrupt my education, again, determined as I was not to leave Toulouse without a diploma. I stayed, counting the days to my freedom and planning to leave as soon as feasible after exams.

The next day I went to Ligny for my usual Monday classes. I feared that, during my absence, she would rummage through my things. I was 23 years old, yet I had no privacy. I ended up taking all my notes with me, along with the letters from my close friends. In those letters we had shared our dreams and our insecurities, explored the meaning of life and spoken of our future. My correspondence was very important for me as these friends were close to my heart.

During my lunch hour at school, I went into the kitchen, walked over to the stove, removed the cover and, one by one, burned my notes and the letters from my friends. With each flame a part of me went up in smoke. It was a searing, devastating experience. I was badly shaken. That's when I realized that anyone can lose his mind if enough pressure is put on him. I left the kitchen totally drained. After that episode only my determination to finish school kept me going.

Happily, I passed everything and so earned my *Licence-es-Lettres* in record time. Most students took four, five or even six years. I did it in three, taking two major exams each year. I admit that I was very proud because I knew I had achieved a lot by dint of determination and hard work.

During my last summer in France, M. Ferran, one of my professors, recommended me for a substitute office job since the regular secretary took a whole month's vacation. I ended up working for six weeks at an affiliate of Westinghouse called Schneider-Westinghouse while I also prepared my documents for my immigration to America.

While there I had an interesting experience with my co-workers— the secretary and a young man from a Catholic family of modest means. The eldest of nine children, he had his *Baccalauréat* but because his family needed the income from his job his dream of going on to the university was shattered. He looked up to me because I had just finished my degree. We became friends. It also became clear to me that he and the secretary were not on good terms. I quickly discovered the reason. He had a degree and she did not, and so he looked down upon her as socially inferior. The secretary had discerned his hauteur and had responded in kind. It took me, a stranger, to rapidly change their relationship. By the end of my first week I had managed to get these young people to make peace and be more accepting of each other.

One day, in the course of our conversation, he mentioned that anyone who is not baptized goes to hell. That took me by surprise. I looked at him and told him that I was not baptized. His face sank. Finally, he managed to say in a low voice, "But you are much too nice to go to hell." I trust the Catholic Church has changed its teachings since then.

Summer 1952 in Bayonne in the dress I made.

After my job ended, I went to a two-week summer camp for students on the Silver Coast in Hossegor near Bayonne. In the fall I worked again for the Librairie Joseph Gibert.

The summer camp deserves special mention. It consisted of a tent city behind the dunes facing the Atlantic Ocean. I met students who wanted only to sleep with me. I was not interested, still believing in romantic love. In order to do some sightseeing, I bought a ticket for the bus to Bayonne, a town near Biarritz, the famous resort on the Atlantic coast. With the little money I had left I bought a pound of apples at the market as food for the day and took lots of pictures, including the one of myself in front of the ocean. (I planned the picture and then asked someone to take it.) On the way back, I hitchhiked as I had no money left.

The most valuable experience I had in Hossegor was meeting a German law student, Franz G. We talked a lot. He was extremely nice and we were able to touch on the difficult subject of the Nazi period and of my suffering at the hands of the Germans and their collaborators. He later sent me some books for the thesis I had planned to write. With the books he enclosed a card that said: "As a token, to make up a little for what cannot be made up for."

I never forgot him, and reconnected with him recently on a visit to Germany.

Aside from the Rosicrucians, I was obviously surrounded by Christians and by Christianity. I had been looking for meaning after the long years of religious persecution and found it nowhere. As mentioned earlier, I read books on Hinduism and Buddhism. I read the book on Jesus written by Ernest Renan, who was a free thinker and not in line with traditional Christian teachings. Far from it. All this was part of exploring life and its meaning. I also hated being Jewish, not because of its teachings, but because I hated being persecuted. Even today, I don't think that a merciful God wants those who believe in Him to be gassed for *Kiddush HaShem* (for the sanctity of His name). It does not make sense to me. I believe in freedom and ethics and goodness. Now, looking at other religions, I feel that Judaism can stand up to any faith, but at the time I didn't see it that way.

Rereading my diary, I came across comments made on this subject by people who were my friends. Aline said to me once that my being Jewish will cause people to step away (*"prendre un recul"*) and another said that being Jewish is a blemish (*"une tare"*). This from friends!

Surrounded as I was by Christianity and Catholicism in particular, its mysticism and spirituality appealed to me. One of my good friends became a Carmelite nun. Fortunately, I did not convert, but I recognize now that there were subtle and not so subtle pressures to do so. Of course, my mother's presence put a break on those ideas. I was not sure what I would do away from her.

Once in the States I corresponded with a former fellow student who was a priest. Abbé Schildt was much older than the rest of us, having been a chaplain in the French Army during the war. He graduated before I did and went off to Ireland to teach at St. Patrick's University in Dublin. With him I was able to express my reservations. There was much I could not accept in Catholicism from the Immaculate Conception to the Ascension and more. Of course now I know more and I understand more about both Judaism and Christianity and have been able to develop my own ideas.

The exchange with Abbé Schildt was helpful in clarifying my own ideas. He agreed that, under the circumstances, it was better for me to stay where I was religiously. I am very glad I did! The truth is that it has taken me a very long time to accept myself. I think the damage done to my self-image early in life left lasting marks. This becomes particularly obvious when I speak to American Jews who did not experience what I did.

As the time for my departure drew near, my mother helped me get ready for my emigration to the States. She sewed on buttons and mended my clothes. Her motivation was not because she cared for me or how I looked. Rather, she lived for the gallery. "I don't want Aunt Anny to say that I sent you to her with torn clothes," was her comment.

I left for the United States in early November. I stopped in Paris for a couple of days to say good-bye to old friends, especially Jacques, who was not doing well by then. I said goodbye to Leon and to another friend, Jean Jacques, who promised to follow me to America. That left me confused as to his intentions and I ended up writing to him *"pour en avoir le coeur net"* (to be clear about his feelings). I needed to know whether he was serious about me. He was not.

A well-known French poet wrote *"partir, c'est mourir un peu"* (to leave is to die a little). As my ship left Le Havre on November 14, 1952, I felt a piece of me stayed in France. I had become a French citizen, I had a French education and, although I had experienced much suffering and persecution in that country, I felt French. Now I saw myself as the wandering Jew all over again.

The college graduate, Toulouse, 1952.

These thoughts tempered my sense of adventure. With my mother still in France because her Romanian quota was slower than my Austrian quota, with my thesis topic in my pocket bringing with it the right to more scholarship money, I was likely to come back to France once I mastered English and got to see America with my own eyes. At the same time, I was ready to date and to think about the next phase of my life: marriage and children.

America

A NEW LAND

The *S. S. Liberté* pulled into New York harbor on November 20, 1952 after a stormy crossing. Aunt Anny picked me up at the pier of the French Line.

Among my first impressions of America was that children from every social class were warm in cold weather, each wearing a snowsuit. Having always been cold during my youth, the fact that it didn't matter whether you were rich or poor, childen were kept warm. This truly affected me. I also sensed a greater feeling of public trust and a decrease in the red tape that was so endemic to the French bureaucracy. It amazed me. And the third thing that struck me was that Americans had the same frame of reference that I was accustomed to in Europe. A handshake had the same meaning; 2 + 2 was four every day, and did not change with changing times or political administrations. American civilization was essentially the same as the European, but with a higher standard of living that I found easy to get used to..

It was a good thing I had my French education. When I left, I continued to get my scholarship from the French government, but I left that money with my mother for her living expenses. This angered Huguette, who expressed her annoyance to me. With my professor's blessings, I had a subject for my doctoral thesis and hoped to do research. But Aunt Anny was in no mood to send me to school. In fact, she was a bit leery at first, lest I become a burden, and she made that quite clear to me. There were many horror stories of orphaned children brought to America by kind relatives—who then disappointed them. Eventually, I earned Aunt Anny's respect and we became good friends.

Initially, I spent a week in Aunt Anny's small apartment on West End Avenue and 72nd Street. She then helped me find a furnished room on the Upper West Side of Manhattan. Two weeks after landing, through my uncle, I had a job as a file clerk for minimum wage—$1 per hour. This was quite a letdown after all my academic achievements, but I accepted it as the price to pay as a new immigrant because I wanted to be self-supporting.

During the week at Aunt Anny's, I gained 10 pounds because Aunt Anny, who was a wonderful cook, kept offering more and more food. As a result, I began to skip lunches to catch the lunchtime concerts of Baroque music at Trinity Church, at the foot of Wall Street. In addition, once I started school, I missed three dinners a week, which also helped keep me trim.

I had to get used to American English (since we were taught British pronunciation in France). In order to perfect my English, in February I signed up for a course for foreigners at Hunter College.

Then the news arrived that my mother had gotten her visa and was coming to America. Huguette had written that my mother couldn't stay alone, and so, as a dutiful daughter, I had to accept her as my roommate. To prepare for her arrival, I rented a furnished apartment on 88th Street and Amsterdam Avenue. My life in hell resumed soon after.

In May 1953, when my mother arrived, she noticed the closeness that had developed between Aunt Anny and me and became insanely jealous. Once again, since I was forced to live with her, I was exposed to her volatile moods. But this was not to last for long.

In August of that year I met Steven Cord, my husband-to-be, and six months later, in February, 1954, we were married. At least my mother had one of her wishes granted: I was marrying a Jew. Then she wanted to know what my hurry to get married was all about. Maybe she didn't realize it, but I was already 25.

When Steve came to tell her he wanted to marry her daughter, my mother told him that I did not have a dowry. Of course he already knew that. To me who had seen European Jewry wiped out no matter what their economic position, money was not as important as education, because if one had an education one could always make a living. My mother, on the other hand, was still living in a pre-war frame of reference where a dowry was the most important thing in a prospective

Anna Freudenheim, Aunt Anny, in New York.

Alfred Freudenheim in New York.

bride's possessions. Mama was greatly relieved when Steve did not care about a dowry. She immediately gave us her blessings. After that, however, things deteriorated.

My mother wanted to delay the wedding until she found a job and was able to save enough money to pay for it. Instead, I took matters into my own hands and started planning the wedding. Aunt Anny offered to pay for everything. She got in touch with my future mother-in-law and called my mother to report back to her. Well, that did it! My mother accused her of stealing her child. My mother's former passionate love for Aunt Anny now became equally passionate hatred. After the wedding, my mother made me swear never to see Aunt Anny again. She would not allow us to leave her apartment until we did. After squirming, hemming and hawing for a while, I finally gave in—and continued to see Aunt Anny anyway.

Still, I was uncomfortable, for an oath is an oath. I ended up writing about this dilemma to Abbé Schildt, my friend the priest. He wrote back that an oath is only valid if it is freely given. An oath given under duress is meaningless.

I felt much better after that.

My mother continued to cause me lots of grief. During my first year of married life, her harassment gave me a bad case of boils. I was working in a fancy piano showroom on West 57th Street, when she showed up drunk and publicly humiliated me. Never again did I let her find out where I worked.

I stopped communicating with her after that. I was already married, and so had options. Steve was supportive of my decision and never tried to interfere. I tried to shield him, and later, my children, from her.

Her gynecologist said her behavior was a result of menopause and recommended a D & C, a procedure that cleans out the lining of the womb. When nothing changed after the surgery, he referred her to a psychiatrist who diagnosed her emotional instability. He said that if we were to put her in a mental institution it would be the end of her, but because she was not suicidal she really didn't need to be institutionalized. I agreed.

About two years after Steve and I were married, my mother moved to Boston. She joined an Orthodox synagogue and resumed a more traditional religious practice. She also trained as a licensed practical baby nurse and supported herself that way until she was 61. That year she had surgery for a detached retina and was no longer allowed to bend or lift heavy burdens. She managed on social security, a small pension from the French government (she retained her French citizenship) and some help from Steve and myself.

Years later, shortly before Yom Kippur, I suggested in a phone conversation that, since they were both getting on in years, she and Aunt Anny should reconcile. It was time to make peace. Her reaction was to ask me if I was seeing Aunt Anny. I lied and said no.

Later, she invited my children to spend time with her, alone, and I said no. When they were older, they themselves limited their relationship because of their own experiences with her.

My mother died in Boston at the age of 87, a lonely, bitter woman. She wanted love more than anything else, but never realized how she pushed everyone away from her.

Steve had a business degree and worked as a customer service representative for Schick, the shaver company. One of his duties was to answer people's letters—on paper. When I met him, he worked as a sales representative for Boston Gear Works.

For our honeymoon, we decided to go to Williamsburg, Virginia. It was a funny place for me, the way the Cloisters was funny. The Cloisters is a museum in Fort Tryon Park in northern Manhattan. The medieval structure was imported from France and rebuilt stone by stone. It had glass enclosures, central heating and piped-in Gregorian chants. After seeing the beautiful, weather-exposed cloisters in Moissac, Carcassonne and Toulouse, the idea of a glass-enclosed cloister struck me as very funny. In Williamsburg I found it amusing to see that what Americans thought were quaint antiques were items still being used every day in Europe.

Because Steve was looking to make a career change, on the way back to New York we stopped in Washington, just north of Williamsburg to check on job opportunities at the Department of Labor. After exploring different fields, Steve decided to become a teacher and applied to Columbia University Teachers College to earn a master's degree and obtain his teacher's certification. They accepted him with the proviso that he make up an undergraduate deficiency in American history. He took the two courses during the summer while working. Then he attended school full-time while I worked. He paid his own tuition from savings and a small inheritance from his Uncle Louis. I earned enough money to support us in a very modest lifestyle.

Steve earned his master's degree in 1955 and got a job teaching high school in Hastings-on-Hudson. We moved to Yonkers and rented three rooms on the second floor of a private house. By then I worked for the Vick Chemical Company in New York and commuted by train. We bought furniture, a car, and saved our money for a trip to Europe.

I encouraged Steve to get his doctorate. I, too, continued my education by taking courses in British history, American history and literature at Hunter College in New York. I was still aiming for my own Ph.D.

When we went to France in 1956, I visited old friends and exposed Steve to Europe; he had never been there and enjoyed the trip very much. And when we got back, we started a family. Emily was born in October 1957 and was followed by Louise in November 1959.

Eventually we moved to a middle-income co-op in Riverdale. Steve continued to teach at Yonkers High School of Commerce while taking classes at Columbia. He earned his Ed.D. and in 1962 got a teaching position in Pennsylvania at Indiana State Teachers College, now Indiana University of Pennsylvania. He taught in the History Department and I taught French and German in the Foreign Language Department.

For the first time in my life, my family was financially comfortable and complete. Our son, Daniel, my youngest and last, was born in 1968.

During Steve's sabbatical in 1970-71, I took an unpaid leave of absence and together we spent the entire academic year in France. That trip made me realize that America was now truly my home. I placed our daughters in French public schools while tutoring them in French and helping them with their homework. In keeping with my own language learning experience, I believed in total immersion. By the end of the year both girls functioned well in French and were able to keep up with their school work. All three of my children, now grown, are well-educated, married and with children of their own. Above all, all three are good and caring human beings and all three are wonderful parents, a fact of which I am very proud.

By 1975, because of departmental politics at Indiana University of Pennsylavania, I began to suffer from stress and looked for a change. A securities broker who came to our campus to help professors with their retirement planning and investments became a friend of mine. To my surprise, he invited me to work with him.

I took an unpaid leave of absence to make sure I could handle the work and took the needed exams to become a licensed securities broker and insurance agent. In 1984, I earned the CFP designation.

(l-r) Otto Steinmetz, Leon (Wodo) Vermont (né Wodowski),
Jacques Hepner and me in Paris, 1956.

Eventually, I moved to Columbia, Maryland, and built my own financial planning practice. I continued to service my Indiana clients, many of them friends or former colleagues.

I worked in that field for 29 years, retiring at the age of 78.

Now I devote myself to writing and lecturing on the evils of religious and racial discrimination, and political persecution because never again should mean never again for anyone.

In my desire to share my hard-won insights with the young people I address in schools and churches, I wrote down 10 lessons from my life.

1. What you think matters; your thoughts have consequences that can be positive or negative depending on their nature. Remember that thought precedes action. Check your belief system. Is it life enhancing or life destroying?

2. Hatred begets hatred. Contempt begets contempt. The best definition of love is acceptance. If you want peace and love in the world, send out thoughts of peace and love. Hatred, like love, is an attachment: it ties you to the object of your hatred just as love ties you to the object of your love. Let go of hate and you will be free.

3. The creative energy that is in you is also in your fellow man. If you truly recognize that, you won't hurt another in deed, word, or thought, as that would be like hurting yourself.

4. Honor the sanctity of life in yourself and in others. Do not defile your body through destructive behavior. Treat it with respect as the temple that houses your spirit. It supports you in achieving your goals.

5. Our shared values allowed us to build a strong, diverse country with opportunities for all. Let us emphasize our common humanity and not our differences. Enjoy these differences; they add spice to life. They enrich us. Do not use them as an excuse to separate us.

6. Take advantage of the wonderful opportunities society offers you. Most especially, honor your teachers, and make the most of your schooling. Knowledge is not enough. Develop the heart along with the mind. This does not happen by itself. And remember that everything can be taken away from you, except what is in your heart and in your head.

7. Take responsibility for your life. Do not blame other people or circumstances for failure. It is not poverty or trauma that leads to moral decay, but lack of values.

8. Low self-esteem leads to alienation and anger. Raise the sense

of your own worth through achievement.

9. Confronting challenges makes us stronger and builds character.

10. Pierre Curie said: We must make of our life a dream, and then turn that dream into reality. First comes the vision.

Several years ago, during a visit to the Holocaust Memorial Museum in Washington, D.C., I strolled over to the Tidal Basin that graces the Jefferson Memorial. I sat on a park bench admiring the reflection of the trees in the smooth, mirror-like surface of the water, when a seagull planted itself squarely in front of me and looked me straight in the eye. The bird stood there quietly for a very long time and it felt as though she was a messenger from another world. I looked at the snow-white bird, I gazed at the deep blue sky, I admired the glowing fall colors and I was filled with profound gratitude for the gift of our beautiful planet and our wonderful America.

About the Author

Edith Mayer Cord is a successful financial advisor and educator who fled from the Nazis during her childhood in Austria. Born in Vienna between the wars, her parents struggled to raise their children and then had to run for their lives, first to Italy, and then to France. Edith's father and brother were caught and murdered in Auschwitz.

Edith and her mother struggled to survive in hiding. After the war, Edith needed to overcome a dysfunctional family life while coming to terms with the Holocaust. She dedicated herself to pursuing her education under any and all circumstances.

As she says, "My life is my triumph, and if I can overcome, so can others."

A mother of three, Edith is a grandmother of seven, who is now retired and devotes herself to writing and speaking about her experiences in order to inspire others.